MW01714711

For
Fred and Maud Bruemmer
with very best wishes—

[illegible]

Contents

Also by Hanns Ebensten

PIERCED HEARTS AND TRUE LOVE
An Illustrated History of European Tattooing

ALL PLAY, a novel

VOLLEYBALL WITH THE CUNA INDIANS
And Other Gay Travel Adventures

THE SEALS ON THE ICEPACK
And More Gay Travel Adventures

TRESPASSERS ON EASTER ISLAND
Explorers, Whalers, Slavers, Adventurers, Missionaries, Scientists and Tourists, from 1722 to the Present Time

THE QUEST FOR DIBBISH
And Other Tales of People and Places

ISBN Number 1-57087-647-9

Library of Congress Control Number 2004102859

Professional Press
Chapel Hill, NC 27515-4371

Manufactured in the United States of America
04 05 06 07 08 10 9 8 7 6 5 4 3 2 1

Home and Abroad

Hanns Ebensten

— 1 —

Awakening in Great Zimbabwe

I was an art student in Johannesburg in 1939, after having arrived in South Africa from Germany with my parents four years previously. I was sixteen and quite innocent. Neither my father—who had married late and was then in his late sixties—nor anyone else had explained the "facts of life" to me; my mother was far too genteel and embarrassed to do so, and my school fellows treated me as a sissy freak and did not share their licentious tales with me.

The German emigrants—mostly but not all Jewish—kept together, and my mother bought her meat, fish, vegetables, groceries, bread and cakes from shops owned by emigrants and rarely spoke English. Her dressmaker was from Berlin, our shoemaker and radio repairman were from

Bavaria. All my parents' friends were German and we were entertained in their homes or they came to ours for *Kaffee und Kuchen* in the morning or afternoon, or for lunch or dinner.

I had almost no companions of my own age and only one of them was a girl. Lixi Mey was the daughter of one of my mother's regular bridge ladies, a couple of years older than me and also an artist. She had no boyfriends and went around with a group of girls and her former hockey teacher. When she had a meal in our home my mother was polite to her but always picked up the cup or glass and the knife, fork and spoon she had used before our native "boy" cleared the table, and took them to the kitchen and scrubbed them with scouring powder and washed them under very hot running water. It was very strange, but when I asked her why she did that, she would not explain. "I can't tell you, but when you are older you will understand what she and her girlfriends and that hockey teacher do."

When we had arrived in Johannesburg my parents could not aspire to live in the elegant Northern Suburbs where the houses stood in large gardens and had swimming pools and tennis courts and needed a staff of eight or more native "boys" to be properly kept up. We lived in Bellevue East, a considerably more modest suburb but also on high ground north of the city's business center, where other emigrants from Europe had settled; but my school, although it was only just over a mile from our house, was down in Bezuidenhout Valley where "poor whites" resided, people "we cannot possibly know," who did not speak nice Oxford English but a sort of bastard language mixed with that dreadful Afrikaans that was a disease. There, also, were the *Ostjuden*—lower-class Jews from Russia and Poland and Lithuania "and other such horrible places," whose forebears had come to South Africa in the 1880s, attracted by the diamond and gold discoveries, but who had failed to prosper. My parents despised all this "riff-raff" and did not want their precious son to associate with the sons of plumbers and truck drivers and miners from whom, my father often told me, I would learn bad habits and ugly words.

My only friend at school—I never dared to bring him home—was a ruffian named Percy Barkham. I was greatly puzzled one day when he said, "*Ach, mann,* I'm so scared; I'm going to be very sick but I can't tell my ma and pa." I advised him to go and see a doctor.

"*Ach, mann,* a doctor can't help me. I'm so ashamed. A soldier made me do something disgusting and now I'm going to be very sick."

I could not think what it could possibly mean and worried about it; but two days later Percy was again his usual cheerful self. "I'm O.K.! I'm not going to be sick, I asked about it; it's like not hatching a chicken in your guts after you've eaten an egg!"

I had not the slightest idea what he was talking about.

Among my parents' acquaintances was a Mr. Cossman who owned an office equipment and stationery store. My father bought all his office supplies from him and when I began my art course I went there for my paper and paints. He was a bachelor in his late twenties whose parents had unwisely remained in Germany and were suffering under the Hitler regime. My parents thought he must miss his family and often invited him to have wholesome dinners with us. He was in superb physical condition, boxed twice a week at a gymnasium and at weekends drove into the country to hike and swim. He had strong, muscular, sun-tanned arms and large brown hands with spatulate fingers. When he sat next to me at dinner he stepped on my feet under the table; I wondered why he did that but never told my parents about it.

I was effeminate and had never learned to whistle or throw a ball; I played no games and instead read those books that my parents permitted me to read and enjoyed sewing and mending my clothes. My parents never showed me that they were disappointed by my lack of interest in sports but encouraged me to make a friend of Ulrich Cossman who, they told me, would be like an older brother to me.

But I was somewhat uneasy about Mr. Cossman, although I did not know exactly why. When my mother's friend Lilly came for *Kaffee und Kuchen* one day, I happened to have just returned home after buying my pads of watercolor paper and Winsor & Newton paints and boasted that Mr. Cossman had given me a big reduction in price. While my mother was in the kitchen making coffee, Lilly said to me, "When you see your kind Mr. Cossman next time, please tell him how ill Lilly Weinstein looked when she came out of Dr. Botha's expensive private clinic where she had a dreadful time, and how poor she now is—" and when I passed on that cryptic message, Mr. Cossman said, "Oh, I'm so sick of women; it was all her fault and I'm not giving her a penny!"

The German emigrant community was not large and I heard rumors—that apparently did not reach the ears of my mother and father—that Mr. Cossman secretly made extra copies of confidential documents that mining and commercial firms gave him to be duplicated on his machines. He then sold the copies to their business competitors. I heard also that he was being blackmailed for a substantial amount of money by a Boer farmer to whose son he had done something nasty. But in my parents' eyes Mr. Cossman could do no wrong. He never failed to bring my mother flowers or a box of chocolates when he came to dinner. He was so kind and so democratic and took the rough, uneducated driver of his company's delivery van with him for weekends in the country, along with poor working-class boys whose parents—if they *had* any!—could not afford to provide them with such treats. He was a man one had to admire. What a good older, wiser brother or friend he would be for me! My parents' great fear was that I might "fall into the wrong hands," by which they meant the hands of girls with nasty painted fingernails or, even worse, experienced older women. They were glad I took no interest in girls (except for that impossible but "safe" Lixi Mey) and began to spend more time outside my home with that charming, athletic, good-looking Mr. Cossman.

But my friend Lixi, who also bought her art supplies from him, was wiser and always referred to him and Piet, the driver of his delivery van, as "the devil and his apprentice."

One evening after dinner, before Ulrich left—he never stayed long after the meal and always said he had to go back to his office to check on the day's sales or the inventory—my father asked him if he would take me along on one of his trips into the countryside. "It will do the boy so much good to walk and swim and learn about camping in the wild and so on." Ulrich was not overly enthusiastic, nor was I, being afraid to do something I had never done before and of being with strange boys who were used to roughing it; but a few days later Ulrich invited me to go along with him the next weekend to the Vaal River and told me what to wear and what to bring with me. He was taking three boys who worked in a builder's supply warehouse and we were to travel in his car; the tent and all the camping gear would be in his van, driven by Piet. I was proud that he had agreed to include me in the trip but had considerable misgivings. It would all be so uncomfortable, so strange without a bathroom and running water, no toilet, no electric light. However, it would be an adventure and I decided to make the best of it.

"This is the first time you have been away from your home since we sent you to Dr. Hermann's Kinderheim at Wyck-auf-Föhr in the summer of '28," my father told me; "but now you are sixteen and almost grown up and your mother and I think you are ready to go out into the big wide world, and we trust the kind Mr. Cossman to look after you." He explained that I must learn that the world consists of rich and poor and I must be as polite to Mr. Cossman's rough young friends as to people of our own class. "But if they do anything you do not like or use bad language or swear, just ignore that and always remember who you are." I promised to do so.

Although the bell tent was large enough for all six of us, Ulrich and Piet slept in the van. I tried to help the others to put up the tent but was awkward and useless; the boys were experts at it. Ulrich was very capable and directed us all to clear a cooking site and collect dry wood for the fire. He showed me how to help him and Piet prepare a meal. He passed out toilet paper and flashlights and boxes of matches and rubbed us all with insect repellent. I need not have been afraid of his warehouse boys; they were quite amiable and did not use bad language or, when they started to swear, quickly stopped themselves. I sensed that Ulrich had instructed them to be gentle with me. After all, I was an art student and lived in Bellevue East! It was Piet the van driver who did not behave at all as I expected a humble employee to do. He was unpleasantly familiar with Ulrich and I could not understand why his boss put up with such uncouth behavior.

How weird it was, to sleep on the ground wrapped in a blanket! The other boys showed me how to dig a "hip hole" to make myself more comfortable, and to walk some distance from the tent with my flashlight, toilet paper and the box of matches with which to burn the paper after having used it and to squat down behind a bush. Life in the army must be like this, I thought, and hoped that I would never have to be in the army.

Next day we all swam across the Vaal River from the Transvaal to the Orange Free State and back, not an achievement like crossing the Hellespont from Europe to Asia but at least into another province. It gave me considerable satisfaction that I could do it, though I was much slower than the others. I began to be able to give more efficient assistance with the camp chores and, on the last day, to take down and neatly fold the tent and stow the gear in the van. I even disliked Piet less than before. Altogether, I felt that I had not been a nuisance to Ulrich and had acquitted myself reasonably well, and in this I was proved to be correct, because a month later he asked my parents to let me go away with him again for an easy climbing trip in the Magalies Mountains near Rustenburg, a three-hour drive from Johannesburg. My father was delighted. "Cossman is beginning to make a man of my son!" he told all his friends and business associates.

On this trip we would not be camping but staying with Ulrich's friend, a Miss Mollie McGregor who had a farm near Rustenburg and had invited him and his friends to stay with her. My mother did not like the sound of this, but one of my father's business associates knew a lawyer in Rustenburg, Mr. Herbert Cranko, and my father telephoned him to enquire about this woman. "Yes," said Mr. Cranko, "Mollie McGregor is a well brought-up lady of a good Scottish family and one of the largest landowners in the district. Her apples are famous and she and her friend Helen are quite respectable, if a little eccentric." Thus reassured, my parents had no objection to my going there.

The guest accommodations at the farm were limited, so only Ulrich, looking devilishly handsome in very brief white shorts showing his strong, tanned legs, Piet the "devil's apprentice," an orphan boy with acne and the forefinger of one hand cut off at the knuckle, and I drove there in Ulrich's car. Miss McGregor led Ulrich, Piet and the orphan boy to settle into her guest rondavel, a circular brick house with a straw roof built to resemble a kaffir kraal. It was a short distance from the farmhouse, where I was to sleep on a cot in the sitting room.

Mollie and her friend certainly were eccentric, as Mr. Cranko the lawyer had told my father. They wore high riding boots, breeches and hacking jackets, their hair was cut short like men's, and they smoked *pipes*! But they were both most welcoming and hospitable and gave us good meals. After dinner they played poker with Ulrich and Piet and the orphan, but I did not know the difference between knaves, queens and kings, nor that between hearts, diamonds, spades and clubs, so felt very much left out and very stupid.

Miss McGregor was celebrated not only for her apples but for her and her friend Helen's audacity in having gone uninvited to a garden party in honor of Her Royal Highness Princess Alice the Countess of Athlone, who had come to Rustenburg for one night to meet the English farming community. The mayor of Rustenburg and his lady wife and the city commissioners had decided that they could not invite Mollie and Helen to this party, despite the fact that Mollie was well respected, one of the largest landowners, and always a generous supporter of any charity—but their *clothes*! And those mannish haircuts! And those pipes that were never out of their mouths! No, it was unfortunate, but they could not send them invitation cards. The day of the garden party came, the functionaries greeted the guests, and to their horror Mollie and Helen drove up to the gate in their disreputable old car, dressed as usual in breeches and men's hats. They could not be turned away, and as soon as the princess saw them she ran towards Mollie and cried, "Mollie—you here!" and Mollie cried, "Alice—after all these years!" and they embraced. They had been at school together.

We drove in Ulrich's car from the farm to the base of the Magalies mountain range. He had brought along bottles of water and made us all drink a lot before we began the climb because the bottles were too heavy to be carried up with us. Instead, he handed out plenty of *mebos* which we stuffed into all our pockets. "But don't finish it all on the way up," he warned us. This dried apricot paste is a South African culinary specialty, firm yet soft, covered with a white dusting of sparkling salt, wonderfully refreshing and, as Ulrich said, it provides almost instant energy.

The ascent was comparatively easy. We wound our way up grassy meadows which were seldom very steep; occasionally some outcroppings of rocks had to be negotiated. I had worried about being able to keep up with the others, but they never had to stop and wait for me. After three hours we reached the summit and from one of the pockets of his khaki safari shirt Ulrich produced a small round instrument, not much larger than a watch, which measured the altitude. We were 8,124 feet above sea level and the Crocodile River and the Hartebeestpoort Dam were 3,000 feet below us. We had not climbed to the top of Mount Everest, not quite, but it was a formidable accomplishment. We rested for a quarter of an hour, lying flat on the ground with our feet raised, and now Ulrich allowed us to eat the last of our *mebos*—but then, instead of descending by the same route, he made us follow him steeply down into a kloof, a deep, narrow gorge through which a small stream trickled among rocks and at many places formed a waterfall. It was a shorter way, he said, but not as easy as going up. Not as easy was a gross understatement; even Piet and the sturdy orphan boy had as much difficulty as I, and so, after a while, did Ulrich. We had to pick our way carefully down along the edges of the stream or actually jump across it from rock to rock. We became wet and muddy, we stumbled and slid, we grasped the branches of overhanging bushes and trees that scratched our hands. I was no longer shocked when Piet and the orphan cried "Bloody hell!" and "*Gottverdammt*!" and "*Ach*, shit!" as they cut themselves on rocks and blood flowed down their arms and legs. Often we had to help each other by holding hands, and I felt quite sick when the orphan took my hand in his with the finger off. I could well believe that this sinister kloof was the haunt of evil spirits, of malignant kobolds who, as it became dark, would cause us great harm, but it was impossible to climb out of this fearful gorge, its sides were too steep, we had to make our way back to the valley somehow, nor could we proceed slowly and with care because the sun was about to set and in half an hour it would be quite dark. Suddenly Piet gave a shout, but not of anger or pain, and almost fell into the stream as he jumped across it to a tree. "It's a wonderboom!" he cried, and picked one of the big green things that hung from its branches and ate it. "Is it O.K. to eat?" I asked, alarmed. "*Klaar, mann*; it's a wild fig tree," he said, so Ulrich and the orphan also ate some but I pretended to eat one and then threw it away when they did not see me do so; I did not trust Piet and did not want to get sick.

The kloof widened, we could walk reasonably well along the side of the stream, which had almost become a river, and suddenly it was all over. We were in the gentle, cultivated valley. We congratulated each other. "We did well," said Ulrich. "Three hours and twenty minutes up and two hours and thirty-five minutes down."

Back at the farm he knew exactly what had to be done and made us all wash our arms and legs with hot water and vigorously scrub them and put iodine on all our cuts and scratches. When I winced he said, "Don't be a sissy now. I know it stings a bit but it's good for you." Mollie and Helen treated us like heroes. They had cooked a special farewell supper and for dessert each of us had one of their famous apples, sizzling hot from the oven, cored and filled with dates, raisins and nuts.

Then Ulrich planned a far more audacious trip, not another easy excursion to a place only a few hundred miles from Johannesburg but an expedition for real outdoorsmen to another country, Rhodesia, to inspect the mysterious ruins of Great Zimbabwe.

Passports would be required, inoculation against smallpox and yellow fever and tetanus was advisable, Quino-Phasmoquine tablets to prevent malaria had to be taken daily beginning a few days before departure, during the week of the expedition, and for ten days after it. We would travel by train, a long journey across Bechuanaland and with many changes en route. It was an irresistible opportunity, particularly because we were to camp right inside those puzzling ruins. We would be joined by Ulrich's friend Leo, whom I had met briefly and did not much like, although he was always very nice to me. He was younger than Ulrich but a sedentary person and prematurely bald. He was a graduate of London University, a Belt scholar, a sociologist who specialized in African affairs, and a professor at the University of the Witwatersrand in Johannesburg. He had written officially to a former London University fellow student, now employed by the Rhodesian government in its Department of Native Affairs, requesting permission to bring a small group of his students to Great Zimbabwe for two or three nights and to camp inside the ruins so that he and they could fully absorb the mysterious atmosphere of that strange place and conduct their investigations in the best way. His friend Joseph had sent an encouraging reply and would facilitate our visit, providing natives to cook our meals and attend to the camp chores. He looked forward to seeing Leo again and would be happy to be our guide.

My parents were acquainted with Professor Leo Silberman's mother, formerly Miss Hilda Meyer, a great heiress, which impressed them even more than her son's academic qualifications. I could not fail to benefit by traveling with a man so well born and, despite his youth, so well respected. It would be not only an interesting and enjoyable week for me but a valuable learning experience.

"That Mr. Cossman is a bit of a rough diamond," said Mrs. Silberman. "He always strikes me as being rather sinister, with all that mass of uncombed black hair and that moustache and those brooding eyes under his thick eyebrows, but my Leo will take good care of your boy. Leo is a good son: instead of wasting his evenings with silly girls, as other young men do, he stays at home and studies and darns his socks, and if one of his students misses his last bus out to a suburb, he lets him share his bed for the night. He is kindness itself."

This fully satisfied my parents, who gladly allowed me to go off with Ulrich and Leo and their adventuresome young men on this educational visit to explore Great Zimbabwe.

Everyone in South Africa had heard about the riddle of those ruins, and I now obtained all the available information on them, which was not much. It seemed almost as if they were a closely guarded secret. Zimbabwe was the only large stone structure in Africa south of the Sahara and was called Ophir in the Bible. It was from there that King Solomon had obtained his gold, and it was the palace of the Queen of Sheba, who had journeyed up the east coast of Africa to meet him in Jerusalem. Its distinctive, tall conical tower was pictured on ancient Phoenician coins. The travel posters of the Rhodesian government showed the white Queen of Sheba emerging as a phantom from the ruins, with a black man on his knees before her, offering her the gold he had scratched out of the ground. (They served to make the place appealing to treasure hunters and cranks.) In ancient times, only highly civilized white men could have planned and built those massive walls. It was bizarre to believe or even to consider that African blacks, who were advanced in understanding only barely beyond the apes, could have had the ability and skills necessary to build such imposing structures; all they were capable of—and ever had been—was putting up their simple mud and straw huts.

Even the Rhodesian natives did not believe that their ancestors had built those walls and towers, and the Shonas' short-lived and speedily suppressed independent movement in the early 1930s had used Great Zimbabwe as an example of how, since biblical times, white rulers had exploited their land and its people.

There were, the Rhodesian government publications admitted, some authorities who did not agree that Zimbabwe was the Ophir of the Bible and who instead gave credence to the theory that it had been built by Arabs who were known to have sailed down the east coast of Africa since the ninth century in search of gold and other metals—and Arabs, after all, counted as white! In 1911, when the British South African Police rebuilt part of the Great Enclosure walls and the entrance to the ruins that had been badly damaged by treasure hunters, they carried out their restorations in a suitably Arabian style.

The so-called Acropolis, built among large boulders on top of a hill and nearly obscured beneath encroaching trees, was considered to be of almost no interest, although it was there that the explorer Willi Posselt had in 1889 found the carved soapstone birds that had become the symbol of Great Zimbabwe. Instead, it was the vast circular Great Enclosure in the valley, reputed to have been the palace of the Queen of Sheba, that had become well known and was so often photographed.

After many weeks of preparations, having been inoculated and fitted out in accordance with Ulrich's and Leo's instructions, we set out with our new passports and our malaria tablets and electric flashlights for the big adventure. We each carried our own blanket, waterproof groundsheet, tin plate, bowl and cup, our own knife, fork and spoon; but transporting the tents, lanterns, cooking pots and pans and the camping equipment, which had been so easy in Ulrich's car and van, provided many problems on the trains with all the changes. Ulrich and Leo gave instructions but did little of the work. Mutual animosity soon developed between Ulrich's two uncouth, rough warehouse boys with whom I had been at the Vaal River, and Leo's educated, well-behaved and well-spoken students. "Your bloody professor is making us work like niggers," the warehouse boys complained. I had more in common with Leo's students but felt that I must show my loyalty to Ulrich by taking the side of his ruffians whenever there was a dispute.

Ulrich quickly noticed that we were splitting into two factions. At Bulawayo, where we had to stay one night before taking the branch train to Fort Victoria, two rooms, each with three beds, had been reserved at the Cecil Hotel for what its receptionist called "the young gentlemen," he would not let his three boys occupy one and Leo's three students the other, but made us mix. As always, he was an efficient organizer. He and Leo occupied a separate room.

At Fort Victoria, a big government truck was outside the railroad station to take us and our gear to Great Zimbabwe. There stood Joseph, Professor Silberman's friend and former fellow student, the official of the Department of Native Affairs who held a master's degree in history—and he was *black*, as black as Hades! It was a dreadful shock to me and to the other boys. Leo introduced us to him and we had to shake his hand. I had only once previously shaken hands with a black man, four years before, but that had been the King of Swaziland; I had never known an ordinary kaffir in workclothes who could speak English like a white man. It was an awkward and unsettling new experience for me, as also for the others. "Fancy a bloody kaffir being in charge here," muttered Ulrich's warehouse boys.

Joseph was not actually insolent but he never addressed Ulrich and Leo as "sir" and treated us young gentlemen almost as equals. "The bloody cheeky bastard!" complained the boys. They also demurred about having to sit on the floor of the truck among our camping gear for the uncomfortable half-hour drive to the ruins. "We're being transported like kaffirs!" they said. The landscape was dreary, low brown hills covered with thorn bushes and a few dismal trees, and when the truck stopped outside a high, long curving wall of granite stones and Joseph called out: "Great Zimbabwe!" I was most disappointed. It was just a wall, so roughly made that creepers and trees grew out of the cracks in it. But when we walked through a low, narrow opening I was impressed at the vastness of this Great Enclosure. Soon we were all lost in it because walls ten feet high or more ran in all directions but none in straight lines, and if we had been told to go back to the truck none of us could have found the entrance in the outer wall which was hidden somewhere behind the many other walls. Lower walls looked like immensely long gray snakes coiled in the grass. It was all very weird, a spooky place, but without any houses or remains of houses, no great white queen's palace, it possessed neither the grandeur nor majesty of which I had read. From behind some of the highest curved walls, whose stones were more regularly laid, rose the tall conical tower, the most photographed building of Great Zimbabwe, featured in the travel posters and even on Rhodesian postage stamps and coins.

The natives whom Joseph had recruited carried all our gear from the truck. Joseph indicated the place in the middle of the ruins where they were to pitch our tents on raised, grassy ground near two large trees, and they cleared the area for a campfire. A hundred feet from the tents, behind some bushes, they dug a deep latrine hole and put up a canvas screen around it. "All the comforts of home," said Leo.

By the time we were settled in—the boys and students in the bell tent and Ulrich and Leo in a small tent—and all our equipment had been unpacked and a meal was being cooked and served to us by the natives, all the disagreements during the train journey were forgotten and we were a united group of happy campers. We were still shocked that Joseph, our guide and in control of all the arrangements, was black, but at least he knew his proper place at mealtimes and never sat with us around the campfire but retreated some distance away and ate with the natives who had done the cooking.

After supper, when we were sitting round the campfire drinking hot chocolate—so much better for us at bedtime than coffee, Ulrich always said—out of the darkness the Queen of Sheba slid slowly into the light of the fire, sinuously danced to and fro and lifted her veil. It was one of Leo's students who had made elaborate preparations weeks before for this magical moment; he wore a wig of long fair hair, almost white, a tall golden crown and a white diaphanous gown reaching to his sandaled feet. He had golden chains around his neck and his wrists.

Leo was as much taken by surprise as all of us. He applauded wildly, and so did we, clapping our hands in unison. One of Leo's other students knelt down on the ground before this great white queen, exactly as the black man in the travel posters. The natives had been washing up our supper things and came running from the darkness into the circle of light and danced with joy and waved cooking spoons and ladles, their war cries echoing from the walls around us. The great white queen graciously acknowledged her audience's acclamations, waved to us and slowly moved away to our tent. We finished our cocoa and soon followed, but Ulrich and Leo remained by the fire and smoked.

We scrambled to our places in the tent, with our feet towards its middle pole, and wrapped ourselves in our blankets. It was totally dark and I was very tired but most of the others seemed to be restless. After some time there were sounds as if they were moving around, then I heard noises of sucking and groans as if some of them were in pain. Perhaps they were sick due to the unaccustomed food the natives had cooked, and others gave them assistance but did not want to involve me in their troubles, so I lay very still and heard whispering: "Yes, go on, *mann*, go on," and, "Keep quiet, he's asleep." I slept.

Next morning, after breakfast, Joseph took us on a tour of the ruins.

"First of all, forget about the land of Ophir and King Solomon and his mines and the Queen of Sheba," he began. "I hear that she appeared to you last night; I wish I'd been here to see her. But now I'm sorry to have to destroy your boys' romantic fancies and misconceptions"—oh! how we hated to be addressed as "boys" when it was we who, from earliest childhood, had been taught to call black men like him "boy" and clap our hands to catch their attention—"but I must tell you the truth about this place, and it *is* the truth because the Portuguese came here four hundred years ago and saw it, and traded with the people who lived here and who had built it, and they wrote about it. They had a trading post at Sofala on the coast near where Beira is now, and they visited what was then the powerful Monomotapa Empire, now called Rhodesia. Those Monomotapa people had come here more than a thousand years ago from North Africa, but there were wars and their land was occupied by the Shonas. The Portuguese arrived, traded with them for gold, and saw their cities, the largest and most important of which was this, where the Emperor of Monomotapa lived—a black man, not a white queen! It took the Portuguese only ten to twelve days to walk here from the coast and we have many of their descriptions, which Diego de Aleacora sent to the King of Portugal in 1516, and those of others, who were also amazed by the high walls built without mortar joining the stones, and by the tall tower. Some of those Portuguese visitors even included a priest, who lived here at the royal court. They stayed here for two centuries and the Emperor of Monomotapa ceded all the mines of gold, copper, iron, lead and pewter in his empire to the King of Portugal, and in 1629 he allowed the Christians to build churches and to sit down in his presence—but they did not just sit down; they went about marauding with their guns and destroyed the once prosperous land and the natives fled from them; and by the year 1719 the great empire of Monomotapa was in decay."

He told us that the Portuguese did not believe that the natives had built Great Zimbabwe and other cities they found in the forest; they believed that they had found King Solomon's mines as mentioned in their Bibles, the land of Ophir, the palace of the Queen of Sheba. Although the Emperor of Monomotapa kept up a semblance of civilization, they recognized in Zimbabwe the imposing monument of a vanished glory and when other white men made their way here in later centuries it suited them to believe the legend. In September of 1871, the German explorer Karl Mauch came here and although he is called *the discoverer of Great Zimbabwe,* by then the Portuguese had known the place for three hundred and seventy years and measured and described it in detail. Mauch was industrious and a good observer and his sketch map of the ruins shows them almost exactly as they are today, but he called the natives "the black two-legged rabble that in its proud stupidity thinks itself superior to the whites." He was referring to the Shonas, said Joseph, who had lived and worked there for more than a thousand years and who were his own ancestors. And of course he perpetuated the myth of King Solomon, Ophir and the Queen of Sheba. "You may have heard or read about Karl Mauch. Our history books are filled with praise for him because he said what white Rhodesians want to hear. But you have probably not heard or read about the British archaeologist McIver, who came here in 1906 and whose scientific investigations and excavations proved that Great Zimbabwe was no more ancient than the fourteenth or fifteenth century, was unquestionably African in every detail, and had been the residence of an African king. His verdict brought such a howl of protest from the Rhodesian government and its white settlers that twenty years later the British Association sent out a second expedition, led by Dr. Gertrude Caton-Thompson, who confirmed with her archaeologist insight what McIver had said before her. Her examinations showed that the builders of Great Zimbabwe were Africans, and not under the direction of a so-called white superior race. How different was her report from that of the Ancient Ruins Company that had firmly stated that no natives had ever taken a hand in the building of this civilization! So now, my boys"—oh! that offensively condescending "boys" again—"you know the truth about this place. I am sorry if I have robbed you of your romantic notions."

He walked away from us, deep in thought, and we continued to wander around among the curving walls with Ulrich and Leo.

"That Joseph is really quite clever, for a kaffir," said one of the warehouse boys.

"He is not a kaffir," Leo admonished him. "He is a highly educated man with perfect manners and I would not hesitate to introduce him to my mother."

"*Ja, klaar,* so that she can get him to wash the floors and scrub the toilet!"

"You are very ignorant," said Leo. He told us that Joseph was the oldest son of a Shona chief, that he had been at a mission school where the good fathers had been impressed with his unusual intelligence, and that they had obtained a scholarship for him to go to the London University. "He will go very far. He has political ambitions, but first he must go to jail."

"To jail? But why?" we cried.

"When the countries of Africa become independent, as they will, all their presidents will have received their education at universities in Europe and in their own countries' jails."

His sociology students understood him, but Ulrich's uneducated boys were incredulous; Leo was talking utter nonsense. How could the countries in Africa ever rule themselves—it was impossible, unimaginable. "But the kaffirs can't even read!"

"They can learn, as Joseph did. How long did it take *you* to learn to read and write? Four years, maybe five or six? They can do so, too."

"But they're just ignorant kaffirs!"

"No," said Leo. "It is you who are ignorant. In Africa it is necessary to be colorblind. If you don't like black people you should not live here. Your kaffirs, as you call them, will soon read and write and you will have to learn that by their overwhelming numbers they will sooner or later be your masters, and when Joseph is the president of his country you will be proud that you were here with him."

He was not joking; it was sacrilege. The boys turned away in disgust.

During the afternoon Ulrich took me aside and told me to move my gear into his tent. I had overheard one of the warehouse boys tell him that they had disturbed me in our tent in the night by what he called "our goings-on."

"But what about Leo?" I asked.

"Oh, Leo has made his own arrangements."

After supper, there having been no repeat appearance by our Queen of Sheba, we sang around the campfire and then the boys went to the big tent and I crawled into the small one and soon fell asleep. Ulrich and Leo again smoked by the fire and later I was dimly aware of Ulrich coming into the tent and lying down; but after a while he and I no longer lay side by side in that narrow space but were one, and the earth shook violently beneath us and a screaming wind tore the trees out of the ground and tossed them high into the air and the stars and the moon fell from the sky and I had been brought to life by the finger of God as in Michelangelo's painting of the young Adam and suddenly, amazingly, bewilderingly, excitingly, I knew everything—what Lixi and her girlfriends and the hockey teacher did with their tongues and why my foolish mother scrubbed our knives and forks and spoons after she had used them, and that Percy Barkham had swallowed the soldier's semen, and why the major of Rustenburg did not want to receive Mollie McGregor and her friend Helen at the Princess' garden party, and that Lilly Weinstein had undergone an abortion. I knew now what Ulrich had done with the son of the Boer farmer, and Zeus with Ganymede, and Achilles with Patroclus, and why Alexander the Great went mad with grief when Hephaestion died, and of what Richard the Lion-Heart and Frederick the Great had been suspected. I knew what had been the cause of the sucking and groaning noises in the tent in the previous night. The great mystery of life had been revealed to me and I knew that Ulrich was a bad man and I adored him.

Everything was made clear to me. It had been a heavenly awakening, but how would my life continue, now that it had been so dramatically changed? How was I to behave next morning? How to face the other boys and the students and Leo and Joseph?

The next morning began as any other. The sky became light in the East, the sun rose, Ulrich pulled on his shorts and his safari shirt and went to attend to his ablutions. The natives began noisily to make a fire and cook our breakfast. Everything was as before and only I was different. A sixteen-year-old veil had been removed from before my eyes. The boys came out of the big tent and I knew immediately that they knew what had happened in Ulrich's tent but none of them made a comment or smirked.

But where was Leo? I had assumed that he had spent the night in the big tent with Ulrich's two boys and his three students, but he was not with them. It was odd that no one remarked on his absence. When we sat down to have the hot porridge ladled out into our bowls, he strolled into the ruins with Joseph beside him, and I realized with disbelief that they had spent the night together! How *could*

Leo have done it—with a black man, and one who was so very, so completely black? But Leo was as garrulous as ever, quite unashamed, and sat down to eat with us as if nothing revolting had happened, and Joseph ambled off to eat with the natives, and Ulrich and the boys and the students, who were surely well aware of the situation, talked and joked and behaved as if it was just another morning at Great Zimbabwe.

It was beyond my understanding and I simply had to talk about it. Black men and white men did not sit on the same benches in parks, did not ride in the same buses, did not stand in the same lines at the post office, did not eat together—all that was normal and as it should be, but to *sleep* together? I crawled back into Ulrich's tent where he was sorting his gear. "Did Leo and Joseph sleep together?" I asked, still hoping that I had assumed some horror that had not in fact occurred. "Sure," said Ulrich. I wondered if he would be equally calm and unconcerned if I announced that the world had stopped revolving round the sun. His total acceptance of the dreadful deed amazed and calmed me and, because I now had complete trust in him, I considered Joseph with my newly opened eyes. He was black, yes, unquestionably and completely black, but he did not smell as kaffirs did. He was clean. He was a fine, educated man. It was Leo who now seemed to me to be unpleasantly white, who often had bad mouth odor, who was bald and had a fat belly. I no longer asked myself how could Leo have done it. I thought instead how could *Joseph* have done it? I understood now that I had been indoctrinated to despise people with black skin since I had arrived in South Africa with my parents four years before. At that time, when I was twelve and had met the King of Swaziland in his ceremonial loincloth of spotted animal fur, I had not been revolted by his naked chocolate-colored body but had fantasized about snuggling up to it in his royal kraal. Ulrich's acceptance of and indifference to Leo's choice for a bed partner made me realize that my childish instinct had not been perverse and wrong. Goodness, how much I had learned in one night in the ruins of Great Zimbabwe.

Having given us a history lesson the day before, Joseph now took us for a walk around the ruins and pointed out features that we had not noticed or, if any of us had noticed them, were meaningless to us. First he made us follow him and feel our way through corridors only two feet wide between high curving walls to stand around the conical tower, which stood hemmed in between even higher walls, as if they were intended to protect it. "It is thirty feet high, and those who believe in Ophir say it was a watchtower and those who say the Arabs built it claim that it was a minaret from which the imam called to the people to come to pray to Allah—but there are no steps up to the top, neither outside nor inside; it is not hollow but filled with stones. So what is it? Your guess is as good as mine."

"It looks like a big cock with a hard-on," said one of the vulgar warehouse boys.

Joseph laughed and led us across obstacles created by tree roots and fallen masonry to the enclosure wall where he pointed out its delicately carved bands of geometric decorations. "My people did this, more than five hundred years ago," he told us. "Is this the work of what old Karl Mauch called stupid two-legged rabble? No wonder they were proud when they showed it to him. And in his time, the famous soapstone birds still stood here. When they were cut off their pedestals the Shonas were very angry but were unable to prevent them from being taken away to museums in Capetown, where you will be told that they were carved in biblical times and resemble the sacred bird statues of ancient Egypt. What nonsense!"

Some tourists arrived in the ruins and were displeased to see our tents set up within the Great Enclosure. "How is this possible?" they asked their guide, who explained that it was by government permission. "It is a professor from the university in Johannesburg and his students doing historical research here—" and it was fortunate that, just at that time, most of us were going around with copies of Karl Mauch's sketch plan, which Ulrich had thoughtfully brought with him, and pacing out distances between the stone walls to check on his measurements, which we found to be impressively accurate. The two large trees in the middle of the ruins near our campsite were exactly where he had indicated them. And it was while Ulrich and I with his tape measure were checking the stated circumference of the tower that he told me—oh! so casually—to keep my gear in his tent for another night. I almost burst into tears with relief and pride. My happiness was complete.

In the afternoon the natives who were doing our camp chores proudly brought Joseph a tin bowl with colored beads, most of them green, yellow and white; they had sifted the soil that they had dug up when making our latrine and found these beads in it. Joseph delicately picked them up one by one with his black fingers and dropped them into the pink palm of his left hand and reverently scrutinized them, then effusively thanked and complimented the men.

"So what—they're just kaffir beads," said one of Ulrich's boys.

"You are wrong," said Joseph. "They are not just kaffir beads; they are Chinese and a thousand years old. Chinese merchants came here between the sixth and twelfth centuries, long before the Portuguese explorers, and traded with the Monomotapa people, and gave them these beads in exchange for gold. The museums on Bulawayo and Salisbury will be thrilled to have them."

"How do you know?" asked the unconvinced boys.

"Because Professor Horace Beck, the world's greatest authority on ancient beads, published a study on these *Rhodesian Beads*. So you see, they are literally worth their weight in gold."

Next day the natives took down the tents. We helped them carry all our equipment out of the ruins to the truck and rattled away to the railroad station at Fort Victoria. All of us were well pleased that we had seen Great Zimbabwe, and not merely for an hour or two like the tourists but for three days and nights, living right inside the large walled enclosure; but I was secretly ashamed of looking forward to eating a meal at a table and to sitting on a flush toilet.

Joseph had not only been informative, but at times humorous, and a congenial guide and none of us, I believed, now minded shaking his black hand when we said good-bye to him. He told us that the natives at the ruins would never forget our visit and that of the Queen of Sheba. He hoped Leo would bring us again: "Maybe I'll see her then?" "I am a Jew," said Leo. "Next time I will make an appearance as King Solomon." "And I am a Shona," replied Joseph, "and will be the Emperor of Monomotapa."

Leo and one of his students were staying on a few days in Bulawayo to pursue sociological researches and there were only two rooms for the rest of us at the Cecil Hotel. Ulrich commanded me to share the room with Leo's two remaining students and he shared the room with his two warehouse boys. It was a bitter disappointment. I had learned so much from him at Great Zimbabwe and now I had to learn to master the anguish of jealousy, in addition to being so desperately afraid of returning to my parents and having to answer their questions about my travel adventure and whether I had solved the mystery of the ruins.

Would they realize or sense that I was not their same precious innocent boy but that the gorgeous, exciting Ulrich Cossman had indeed made a man of me, a totally new, radiantly fulfilled young man? That I no longer belonged to them but to him, that my home was no longer with them but, from now on, in his strong, muscular arms?

— 2 —

Five Wonderful Weeks

Unlike the bishop in the first sentence of Norman Douglas' incomparable novel *South Wind*, I did not feel confoundedly seasick on the ferryboat from Naples to Ischia, but the other passengers were infected with misery. They sprawled on the deck "in attitudes worthy of Michelangelo, groaning with anguish; huddled up in corners with a lemon—a prophylactic against sea-sickness, apparently, pressed to their faces; tottering to the taffrail." And, as in the novel, a fat young priest with a face like a full moon was flirting with a pretty peasant boy.

The mainland slowly receded and first the island of Procida and then Ischia became tangible, with its green hills rising to Mount Epomeo. Clusters of white houses appeared, villages along the rocky shores, a castle. The boat entered an almost land-locked circular harbor and was made fast against a stone quay. I had arrived. It was Sunday, August 22, 1954.

I enjoyed the short bus ride from the port along the coast road past gardens and vineyards and smiling sunburnt fisherfolk and peasants. There was, as in *South Wind*, "an air of contentment and well-being; something joyful, opulent, almost dramatic." I had come to the right place.

At the entrance to the village of Forio the bus stopped in a tiny piazza and I asked at the Bar Mimi where I could find Mr. Philip Dakin. An actor friend of mine in London had recommended me to contact Mr. Dakin immediately on arrival and he would find a room for me. He had been a member of an American dance company and when their tour ended in Naples, he had come to Forio for a week's vacation, married a local girl and now ran a restaurant.

No one knew Mr. Dakin, but three small boys who were loitering outside the bar cried "Oh, Signor Filippo, the trattoria—" and fought for the privilege of carrying my luggage. They led me down some steps to a beach of fine white sand, flanked by short breakwaters of rough stones that provided safe anchorage for small fishing boats. At the back of the beach were cavern-like storerooms into which the boats could be pulled in the winter and repaired, and one of these had been converted into a rudimentary eating place whose crudely lettered sign bore the words SATURNINO DI FILIPPO. Philip Dakin remembered my actor friend and was most welcoming. When I explained that I planned to stay in Forio for a month, he knew exactly the house where a clean room with a terrace would suit me and sent one of the hovering boys to take me to it. "For a month's stay be sure to bargain with Signora Morena for the rental," he said, "and when you're settled in, come back here tonight for dinner."

The boy led me to the main street and then up some narrow, tortuous lanes to a moldy wooden gateway in the Via Cesare Piro and called out as we entered a courtyard with a well, flowering plants in pots, and sausages and fish and onions hanging from overhead hooks. Signora Morena came down some stairs, untied her apron when she saw me, obviously a prospective tenant, and watched to see that I did not tip the boy too much for having carried my luggage. Although I spoke almost no Italian and she knew no other language, we had no difficulty in making ourselves understood. She named the price for the room, I explained that I was prepared to pay for a month and expected a reduction. We smiled and argued and laughed and she took me up a stone staircase to show me a room with a large bed—a *letto matrimoniale* made up with clean white sheets and pillows with crocheted borders, a highly polished wooden clothes cupboard, a chest of drawers with a mirror above it, a table and chairs with pretty cushions. A glass door opened onto a narrow terrace shaded by a grapevine. At one end was a washroom that had been added to the old house, containing a flush toilet which the Signora pointed out to me with great pride. Everything was simple but in good taste and perfectly clean. Below the terrace was a vineyard.

We agreed on the price for a month and shook hands. I paid in cash and moved in.

When I returned to Philip Dakin's trattoria, he came out of the kitchen to ask me if Signora Morena's room suited me and introduced me to Gemma, his wife, and her young brother Giocco, a cheerful imp who was the caretaker of W. H. Auden's house. All the six tables were occupied, so Philip pointed to a lone diner and asked me if I would share with him. I told him I would be happy to do so. "He is an American who has dinner here every evening," he said.

In the dim light of the small room, I had taken him for a dark-skinned or exceptionally suntanned handsome Italian, but as we introduced ourselves I realized that he was an American Negro, albeit by no means black. His name was Jeff Jordan—"Jefferson, named for Thomas Jefferson whose slave my great-great-great-grandfather was and who treated him well and freed him, so that he prospered and then himself owned slaves."

When I expressed my shocked astonishment, he said, "Oh, there was nothing wrong with that. After all, African kings and chiefs used to own slaves and sold them to America."

He told me that he had been a district attorney in Chicago but, being possessed of a fine tenor voice, was now living in Florence and training to become an opera singer.

During dinner we quickly established a congenial rapport and then he invited me to join him for coffee at the sidewalk terrace of the Bar Internazionale di Maria on the main street which, he assured me, "is *the* meeting place for men like us"—and so it was, the perfect vantage place from which to watch the fishermen and boys strolling to and fro and preening for the benefit of the foreign visitors at Maria's tables. I left Jeff there and found my way up the dark lanes to number 11 Via Cesare Piro and my *letto matrimoniale,* but had very much enjoyed meeting him and arranged to see him next day. I was quite exhausted. It had been a long, a very long day for me, yet wonderfully successful. I had a good place to stay and would be installed in it for a whole month, Philip Dakin would be my guide and advisor in Forio, and I had found in Jeff an interesting, good-looking friend. Like the bishop in *South Wind* on his first day on the island, I already felt at home there.

After World War II, when I left South Africa and settled in London, I dabbled in art and literature. I designed the decor and costumes for some productions of the Sadler's Wells Ballet Company and the St. James' Ballet Company. I wrote the script and created the costumes for a glove puppet version of *Hänsel and Gretel* which toured schools all over Great Britain. I wrote magazine articles on such diverse subjects as the South African Ballet, Cape Malay Cooking, Zanzibar, St. Helena and Fez. My first book, *Pierced Hearts and True Love,* an illustrated history of the art of European tattooing, surprisingly became a best seller, and my novel *All Play* had the distinction of causing a court action for libel. All this was very gratifying but far from being profitable, and I was not made to starve in a garret. I was thirty years of age and longing to have regular employment and an assured income. Kind friends recommended me to the Society for Hellenic Travel, who hired me to become their cruise director, but until I took up my duties I had a free summer and the equivalent of US$ 280 in savings. What should I do? Where should I go?

"The grand object of travel is to see the shores of the Mediterranean," said Dr. Samuel Johnson. Roger Peyrefitte wrote about "That middle sea upon whose shores men had best expressed their thoughts of beauty and built their noblest temples to the god"—and the country *par excellence* on these shores that has for many centuries attracted to it painters, sculptors, musicians, writers, composers, daubers and dabblers, young hopefuls and old failures, romantics and eccentrics and hedonists is Italy, amidst whose scenery, like the setting for a romantic ballet, and its matchless antiquities under a warm, sensuous sun, the foreign visitor can truly find the legendary *dolce vita,* in addition to viewing and studying its archaeological and architectural splendors. The reputation of the irresistible Italian men, with their charm, lack of sexual scruples and boldness, dates back to the time of the Roman Empire, as readers of Petronius and other writers are well aware. Lonely bachelors and spinsters fill the hotels and pensione for many months and often rent or buy a villa and remain there forever.

So, for me, too, it would be Italy. And while I planned to spend some time in Florence, Milan, Venice and Rome, imbibing art and culture, many friends urged me to treat myself to a month on the island of Ischia in the Bay of Naples. Capri—the fabulous island of the Emperor Tiberius, of *South Wind,* of the novels of Compton Mackenzie, of the Baron Jacques d'Adelsward Fersen—had become vulgar and common, but nearby Ischia was not yet overly commercialized. The poet W. H. Auden had a house there and said that the character of the people seem to have been little affected by political and technological change. Truman Capote had spent a summer there and called it "an enchanted island: water clear as kittens' eyes." In addition to my impecunious actor friend who recommended me to contact Philip Dakin, my mentor Lord Kinross gave me a letter of introduction to an exceedingly rich friend of his with whom he had been at Eton and Oxford, a Mr. Neil Little, who owned a villa near Forio. And the artist Faith Jaques, who had designed the dustjacket for my novel *All Play,* had twice visited Ischia and urged me to call on her friend Umberto di Meglio, who was in charge of tourism for the island and would be most helpful to me. "You'll be very happy there," she told me. "There aren't any boring old ruins to look at, and the island's chief attractions are its wines and its gorgeous young men's muscles." And I had an additional incentive; the admirable Agatha Christie had just made use of a brief holiday in Morocco to provide the setting for her latest mystery,

Destination Unknown, so perhaps my stay in Ischia would inspire me to write a book about it.

Ischia, the Pithecusa, Aenaria or Inarime of antiquity, is approximately six miles long with a circumference of nineteen miles. Its Mount Epomeo rises to 2,625 feet and was an active volcano at a much earlier period than Vesuvius on the mainland. In the year 474 B.C. the island's Greek population fled, fearing an eruption, and further eruptions occurred in 92 B.C. and later—the last in 1302 A.D. The volcanic soil is extremely rich and Baedeker's *Southern Italy* (the 1887 edition of which I took to Italy with me) describes the scenery as being "singularly beautiful." After the fall of the Roman Empire, Ischia suffered many attacks and devastations by pirates and, between 813 and 847 A.D., by Saracen raiders. In 1299, it was united with the Kingdom of Italy.

I had coffee, toast and honey at the Bar Mimi in the piazza and took the early morning bus to Porto, to call on Faith Jaques' friend Umberto di Meglio at his office in the Municipal Building. No wonder she was enamoured of him and planning to visit him and Ischia again. He was a stunningly attractive man in his mid-thirties, wearing black trousers very tight in the leg and crotch, and a heavily starched, white open-neck shirt with its sleeves turned up to show off his muscular and deeply suntanned arms and impressive gold wristwatch, which I took to be a gift from an admirer. He was delighted to hear about Faith Jaques, welcomed me to Ischia on behalf of the municipality, and handed me a telegram that he had recently received from an English visitor to the island and asked me to explain its meaning. It was from a woman who was clearly in love with him and although his command of the English language was excellent and he understood it perfectly, it was his not too subtle way of making me understand that he favored the female sex.

He was gratified to hear that I was on my way to visit the Castello Aragonese—"so few tourists go there," he said—and intended to hike all over the island and explore it thoroughly, with a view possibly of writing about it. "Very good! And I have just what you need for that," he cried, as he ran to another room and returned with a magnificent topographical map of the island, produced by the Instituto Geografico Militare. When unfolded it measured three feet by four, drawn to the scale of 1:10,000, with altitudes, sea depths and all natural features, as well as every building, marked, from churches and large thermal establishments to the smallest farmhouses, every road and mule track and trail, even prominent trees, grottos and caves. The contour lines, especially those of the high, steep cliffs at the island's south coast, gave it an almost three-dimensional appearance. I was overjoyed, it would be invaluable to me on my rambles around the island.

Umberto di Meglio's kindness did not end with presenting me with the map. He said that he was busy that day but asked me to come back to Porto next evening and have dinner with him at an outdoor restaurant that had just opened on the seashore. "And I will also invite another summer visitor, a young German with whom I believe you have much in common."

I walked around the circular harbor, formerly a volcano crater lake that had been connected with the sea in 1856 in order to provide a safe refuge for ships in stormy weather, and past the Villa Reale, which had been presented by the people of Ischia to King Ferdinand II on his opening of the port and was now the Terme Militare for soldiers, sailors and airmen including ailing veterans of World War II. Another thermal bath, the Stabilimente Municipale, oddly shared premises with the post office. The hot saline mud for it was being carried to it from across the street in buckets by relays of boys. A large white villa had a golden cupola; it was the Yacht Club. A pink villa set among dark, sinister trees reminded me of an ominous painting by Arnold Böcklin. It was less than a mile to the east coast of the island, from where a narrow stone causeway led to a large steep rock in the sea on which stood the remains of the Castello Aragonese. At the end of the causeway I paid the entrance fee to the custodian, who sheltered from the sun under a straw roof with half a dozen little urchin boys whom he offered to me as guides. I showed him my Baedeker and told him I did not need a guide. "Yes, you do, Signor," he insisted and told me to make my selection. When I hesitated, he chose one, who skipped and pranced up the trail in front of me. Before the invention of gunpowder the castle was totally impregnable and provided a heavily fortified place of refuge for the islanders during raids by pirates and Saracens. The celebrated Italian patriot, the Marchese Pescara, was born in the castello in 1489 and defended it against the forces of King Louis XII of France. In 1525 Pescara's widow, Vittoria Colonna, famous both for her beauty and her friendship with Michelangelo, retired to it, as did Maria of Aragon, wife of King Alphonso V of Aragon and Naples. After the seventeenth century, it was rarely occupied and became derelict. In the nineteenth century, it was used as a prison.

Nothing except ruined walls remained and it was practically impossible to determine which crumbling structures had been the living quarters of royalty and nobility, the barracks of the defending soldiers, church or chapel, kitchens or stables. The view across the Bay of Naples was spectacular, with the small island of Procida towards the north—its gaunt fortress now served as the chief prison for the criminals of Naples—along the mainland, and to Capri at the southern end of the bay. The bare ground of the platform on which the castello had stood was pitted with small openings. They had been the underground cells of the wretched prisoners, and my little so-called guide ran from one of these to another, and to a third, and beckoned me with unmistakably licentious gestures to follow him down these treacherous shafts into the darkness. If the dashing Umberto di Meglio had offered me the opportunity to follow him, I would not have hesitated a moment to do so, but the dirty little ruffian had not the slightest appeal to me, and I made my way down to the causeway. "Back so soon? Boy no good? Send another boy? No extra charge," said the custodian.

I returned to Porto and took the bus back to Forio, happy to return to my cozy room, rest on the bed during the heat of the day, munch chocolates and grapes, write my journal, unfold my excellent map and study it, fall asleep and dream. Jeff Jordan and I again had dinner at Felippo's trattoria and afterwards chatted intimately at Maria's. He wanted to see where I was staying; we shared the *letto matrimoniale* and almost immediately and without deliberation or discussion fell into the uncomplicated, pleasant habit of spending not only many hours of every day but also most nights together, either in my room or in his flat just off the piazza overlooking the harbor, with all modern conveniences. We both knew that this was merely a mutually satisfying holiday romance, and would not lead to anything more permanent. It suited me perfectly and, I believe, suited him. Forio was filled with men of all ages and nationalities who were drawn there by the local fishermen's well-deserved reputation for being most accommodating, who vied with one another to be hired for an hour's "fishing trip," their traditional way of making erotic assignations; but the arrangement to which Jeff and I had come was more agreeable to us and had for me the additional merit of not depleting my limited funds.

Next afternoon I went back to Porto to meet Umberto di Meglio at his office. He was pleased to hear that I had climbed up to the Castello Aragonese and was taking an interest in his island's history. "We have to pay a custodian, but on many days he doesn't sell a single admission ticket. The tourists who come here only want to lie on the beaches and drink too much. It is most discouraging." I refrained from pointing out that there were certain other attractions, of which he was surely aware, for which tourists came to Ischia.

We walked to the new, elegantly appointed restaurant O'Rangio Fallone under pine trees at the edge of the Punta Molina, where Heinz Helm was waiting for us. I could not imagine why Umberto had said that Heinz and I had anything in common, unless it was the not unusual uninitiated person's misconception that all male homosexuals like each other. We were complete opposites in every way. He had been in the German Army in World War II, I in the British Army. He boasted of Germany's tremendous economic recovery; I felt threatened by it. "Germany is again the world leader in *everything,*" he announced. "Even the Queen of England's cars are Daimlers, not those outdated, slow Rolls Royces." He was outrageously, exuberantly effeminate; I strove to be manly. His hair was long, artfully coiffured and tinted with golden streaks; I had a crewcut. His fingernails were manicured weekly, long and pointed, lightly enameled pink; I was ashamed of my hands and could never stop myself from biting my nails. He wore golden necklaces, chains around limp wrists and ankles, far too many rings.

Fortunately, the meal was served very promptly and Umberto kept the conversation going with tales of some of the curious foreign visitors he had met in his office, of lost or allegedly stolen passports or money and other calamities, of problems resolved and tempers diplomatically soothed. When coffee was set before us, and small glasses of the local grape brandy, he apologized to Heinz and me, saying he had a late business appointment. "I'll leave you together now, but sit here as long as you wish and order anything you like, you are my guests. *Chiao.*" And off he went, having done his duty, as he believed, by bringing two birds of a feather together.

Without Umberto, Heinz and I could talk freely. He told me that I had made a horrible mistake by staying in Forio. I tried to explain that it suited me well, that I had introductions to people there, and had already made some friends.

"No, Forio is *impossible*! There is nothing there! Everything is here in Porto, all the sailors' and soldiers' barracks are here, and bars where they go and one can meet them, and here one can do what one wants and nobody watches and nobody cares. My pensione is *sturmfrei*, the owner is one of us and I can bring back whomever I want, as many as I want, day and night. Oh, Porto is paradise for a dedicated *Soldatentante* like me, because I only do it with men in uniform, like all good Germans, and I'm very successful at it, I assure you. I follow the tradition started by Kaiser Wilhelm's generals and Herr Krupp at Capri in the good old days. But Capri is spoiled now, too expensive, but here in Porto, it's still paradise."

I was also attracted to men in uniform, but wanted to be their friend, their chum, not their old auntie or a substitute for a giddy girl. No, Heinz and I had nothing in common. We parted without regrets at the bus stop.

Now that I was settled in Forio, I walked up the main road towards Lacco Ameno in the afternoon to call on Mr. Neil Little and present my letter of introduction from Lord Kinross. Mr. Little had named his house Casa Meleagro for the Greek writer of the first century B.C. who had not retired to Ischia but to the island of Cos, which it scenically resembled. He expressed his love for boys in the erotic epigrams for which posterity best remembers him.

The house was set back from the road in an extensive and beautifully maintained garden with adjoining vineyard. A servant opened the door and gestured me to go up into a large room where I was disconcerted to find a cocktail party in progress. Mr. Little, a man in his late fifties, detached himself from his guests and greeted me. Neckties were not worn in Ischia except by senior government, police and postal officials, but he did not want to relinquish his Old Etonian tie, that symbol of the British upper-class gentleman, and used it, loosely knotted, as a belt. I handed him Patrick Kinross' letter and explained that I had not known that he was giving a party.

"Oh, all Forio knows that Fridays are my At Home days," he said. "But come and meet everyone."

The notabilities of Forio and its most prestigious summer residents were assembled. Sir William Walton, the English composer, and Herr Hans Werner Henze, the German composer, had villas nearby at Montevergine above the San Francesco beach. Lady Walton assumed the role of the gracious *châtelaine* in Mr. Little's mostly male *ménage.* A chubby, jovial, madly animated woman to whom the other guests deferred, was Anna Maria Mussolini, daughter of "Il Duce," the murdered dictator. The Swedish writer Bengt Söderberg and his French friend Marc lived in an ancient fortified tower. And shuffling unsteadily through the room, slopping the wine in his glass, was a flabby, uncouth monster, supported by a chubby young blond man. This was W. H. Auden, England's greatest living poet, and his lover, Chester Kallman. The gray flesh of his cheeks and neck hung in folds and had a sickly green tinge. Long hairs sprouted from his nose, which bore blackheads as big as flies, and from his large and hideously pendulous ears. His loose lips and the skin around them, as well as his rotting teeth, were discolored by nicotine, as were his fingers. His unpleasantly pale, watering blue eyes were those of a dead fish. When he spoke, too lazy or bored or drunk to do so clearly, a sodden cigarette remained stuck to his lower lip. No doubt the poet talked brilliantly in bed, but how could that nice blond Jewish boy from Brooklyn, New York, spend his nights beside that flaccid, unwashed slug? The mind boggled at the thought of it.

Having read Lord Kinross' letter, Mr. Little placed his hand on my shoulder and led me towards a flight of stairs. "Patrick says you are a writer and an *artist,* so let me ask you for your artistic advice. I want to have a window made in the outer wall of this staircase, so that when I go up to bed I can catch a glimpse of Epomeo—just a small round window. What do you think?"

I said it seemed to be an excellent idea but advised against having a round window. Round windows never look right in houses and resemble ship's portholes. A square or oblong window would be preferable.

"Yes, that had not occurred to me. I will take your advice. How fortuitous that you arrived just in time to give me the benefit of your expertise."

He was playing the role of the genial host.

His Swiss friend, Kurt, was in charge of the bar, where he and I enjoyed a lengthy chat while he adroitly mixed cocktails. When I complimented him on his efficiency, he explained that he had been a bartender in St. Moritz before Neil swept him off his feet and brought him to Ischia for the summer. He was a cheerful, amiable young man; I had made another friend in Forio.

I then began to make explorations with my map and a book on the *Architettura dell' Isola d'Ischia,* whose detailed drawings of the churches and principal buildings I annotated to make a record of the deteriorations since they had been documented in the late nineteenth century. The map had been produced at least twenty years ago and as I walked around the island I revised it by adding many new buildings and some roads. Doing all this provided my rambles with a purpose and gave me a great deal of pleasure.

Forio was very quiet—which suited me ideally but had aroused Heinz Helm's scorn—because the motor road around the island did not enter it. The bus from Porto, having deposited or picked up passengers in the piazza on the edge of the village, then continued up into the hills and high above the south coast back to Porto. But there was always something to do: at least twice a week I visited the post office, a social center where visitors went to meet and exchange gossip and news and to buy stamps and ask for letters at the Poste Restante desk; it was an adventure to wait my turn at the village barber's and instruct him in the art of creating a good crewcut. "You want to look as if you just been released from prison?" he asked. "The good God gave you hair, why make me cut it off?" On Sundays there was either a bicycle race or a display of gymnastics by school children, or everyone followed the mayor and other local dignitaries from shop to shop as they judged the display of local grapes. And it was always a joy to walk to the white stucco fifteenth century church of Santa Maria del Soccorso on the promontory above the sea, whose lower walls were covered with pretty floral tiles and where five sinister black wood crosses in a row flanked the curving ramp leading to the bright green doorway. The Franciscan monks moved about balletically in their corded brown habits, holding the hands of their cherubic little barefooted acolytes and stroking their hair and bestowing kisses on their cheeks and arms. To show their gratitude, the little boys, like puppies, lovingly kissed their monk's hands, as the women of Forio, in their best Sunday black dresses and headscarves, stood by and expressed their admiration and approval.

With Ischia's circumference being barely nineteen miles, I could make easy day expeditions in every direction, mostly on foot and occasionally traveling part of the way by buses, which ran around the island's main road in both directions several times every day from early morning until late at night.

One morning I set out into the hills above Forio, making my way towards the remote Villa Tiromalle of whose beauty I had been told. The scenery was as lush and lovely as one of the early English visitors, George Berkeley, had described it in 1717: "a wonderful variety of hills, vales, ragged rocks, fruitful plains, and barren mountains, all thrown together in a most romantic confusion." Ischia's wines were favorably referred to as long ago as the sixteenth century, and the slopes were draped with grapevines, often contrived into arbors for shade. The volcanic soil and nine annual months of sunshine give the grapes their high quality; the best varieties are the light Forestera and Biancolella and the dark Guarnaccia. Braided clusters of cherry tomatoes, used for sauces to accompany pasta dishes, hung along walls of whitewashed farmhouses. I passed mules laden with baskets of grapes and bundles of vine and olive prunings to feed stoves. It was all most enchantingly rustic.

From across a pasture where goats and sheep were feeding on corn, half a dozen bearded men who were lounging against a large tufa rock waved to me to join them and share the cheese, salami and bottles of wine, which they held up to show me. They lived in caves in the rock and when winter came and it rained they would pull their animals to shelter there with them. Despite their rough, disreputable appearance they were very amiable, laughed a lot, could not understand my map, and invited me rest in the cool shade of one of their caves, but I told them I was on my way to see the Villa Tiromalle, and then to the coast, still a long way to walk. "Villa is for sale; you going to buy it?" they asked and thought it was a great joke. When I offered to pay for the food and wine, they waved me off.

The villa was a dilapidated wreck. I walked down to the road at the village of Panza, a miniature version of Forio, 500-feet above sea level, and then made my way along a road being constructed to reach the Marina del Maronti, the longest beach of the island, facing south and until then inaccessible except by a stiff hike. When the road was completed it would undoubtedly become the most popular beach of Ischia, with all the manifestations of mass tourism, resort hotels, casinos and loud music. It would be the end of Ischia as I was privileged still to see it. It would become a rival to Capri and equally vulgarized. It was sad, but inevitable. Where the construction of the new road abruptly ended, a path led down to Sant' Angelo, a tiny village of the utmost picturesqueness, with a beach uniquely facing both west and east, three small pensione and a thermal establishment catering to Italian and some rare foreign visitors who craved complete isolation. I rested on the terrace of the Pensione Miramar, ordered tea and fell into conversation with a sculptress from Munich who was busily writing postcards to give to the captain of the afternoon boat to Porto; he would buy the stamps and mail them from there. She advised me to walk to a rocky hill which was connected to Sant' Angelo by the strip of beach, where a family living in three caves sold salami and wine under a straw roof. So there, in that romantic setting, like a hermit, I had my second salami-and-wine meal that morning.

The boat left promptly at 3:30 P.M. and took me along the island's south coast, past the deserted Marina del Maronti beach and two miles of steep, high tufa cliffs, around some formidable headlands and the Castello Aragonese to Porto. I arrived back in Forio just in time to meet Jeff for dinner at Felippo's, but was too exhausted to recount all my day's adventures, but happy to share his bed in his flat, so conveniently near the trattoria and sparing me the effort of walking up to my room.

From the boat I had seen the white houses and the church towers and domes of many villages in the hills high above the south coast, so a few days later I made another expedition to inspect these. I took the bus along the tortuously winding road to the piazza of Barano, which commanded a splendid view over a fearful canyon down to the village of Testaccio, with a church painted bright yellow, and to the sea several hundred feet below that. The road from there to Porto wound its way around heavily wooded mountains with almost no farmhouses. Occasionally there was a little whitewashed chapel by the side of the road, which then ran along the bank of a canal. My map marked the Casa di Meglio, which I assumed to be the home of the handsome Umberto's family. An aqueduct on arches crossed the road and I hoped that it dated to Roman times but was told that it had been built in the nineteenth century, had failed to serve its intended purpose, and been replaced by the new canal. Surprisingly, many of its masonry blocks bore decorations in the form of swastikas.

In Porto I had plenty of additions to draw on my map. The town had doubled in extent since the map had been produced and the circular harbor was now completely ringed by restaurants, travel and shipping of ices and small hotels. In a ship chandler's shop I was astonished to see curiously shaped glass bottles suspended from the ceiling among the tackle, three or four or more of them tied together. They were statuettes of Italian kings and queens and generals and statesmen. My favorite was identified on his chest as ALL'EBOE GALLIANO, 1887, with the bottleneck rising from his tropical solar topee. I had never seen anything like them and wondered why tourists had not snatched them up for souvenirs and gifts, but presumably they did not look into a shop selling mundane ship supplies and even if they did, were deterred from buying any of these original bottles because of the difficulty of taking them home. But the thought of this problem did not deter me; I *had* to have some of them, and when the shopkeeper told me their almost ludicrously low price, I selected six. He seemed less pleased than perplexed to have a buyer for them and tied them together with a length or rope for me to carry them away.

The ferryboat from Naples was coming into the harbor and I went to watch the passengers disembark. Only two weeks ago I had arrived there as a tourist–it seemed like a lifetime–and now here I was, a suntanned peasant who had bought bottles to carry back to his vineyard in the hills and fill them with his wine–or so I hoped the tourists would think.

"What on earth are you doing here, and what are all those bottles?" said Heinz Helm as he stepped ashore.

I asked him if he had been to Naples.

"No, only across to Procida for the night."

"Why Procida? The ferry stopped there for a minute when I came here on it, but there doesn't seem to be anything there except that big ugly fortress–and there are no sailors or soldiers for you!"

"Oh, Hanns, you think you are so clever, but you know *nothing*," said Heinz. "That big ugly fortress is a prison full of murderers and thieves and there are more than a hundred armed guards who wear the sexiest tight uniforms and are very, very bored, so once or twice a week I go across there for a night and do it with them. It makes a change from Porto. What are you doing with those bottles? They are quite *bizarre*."

And he went off to the Diana Bar to meet sailors and soldiers.

My daily routine in Forio continued to give me much pleasure and satisfaction. Signora Morena was a most understanding and motherly landlady and when I stayed in bed one day with a sore throat, brought me a pot of chamomile tea sweetened with honey to cure me, and later returned with a large sunflower to cheer me up. She became quite accustomed to seeing Jeff come home with me and treated him as if he, too, was her tenant.

Jeff and I spent long mornings on the beach in front of Filippo's trattoria, where the fishermen's boats were pulled up on the sand. Giocco, the brother of Philip's wife Gemma, who always reminded me of Puck in *Midsummer Night's Dream*, often joined us there, full of salacious gossip about Mr. Auden and Mr. Kallman in particular and the sexual encounters and complications of Forio's summer residents in general.

Jeff's voice trainer, Lala, and her prize pupil, Anette Gibson, also came to the beach most mornings and we sat together and played cards and guessing games. Lala was a somewhat formidable woman in her fifties, good-looking, with a commanding manner but a sense of humor. She had brought little Anette with her to Forio for the summer, to continue her voice training and also to chaperone her. Anette was English, eighteen and sweetly pretty. "Young and dumb," said Jeff. Her father was a rich industrialist and was paying all Lala's holiday expenses. By assiduously preventing anything to harm Anette's singing ability, Lala deprived the poor little rich girl of all holiday enjoyment. The sea was too cold for her, the sun too hot, walking up into the hills to the vineyards was too exhausting. Nothing that might be detrimental to her delicate vocal cords was permitted to enter her mouth. Hot, spicy food aggravated her throat, iced drinks were ruinous, fish and chicken had nasty bones, grapes had carefully to be sucked and the pips spat out. Nuts were especially harmful and even lurked unseen in chocolates and ice cream. There were grave penalties for being an aspiring opera singer. "God has blessed you with a priceless organ; you must do nothing to mar it," she told Anette. Jeff's vocal cords were apparently impervious to all these dangers and Lala rarely chastised him for eating what he wanted. In the afternoons she kept Anette with her in a shuttered room, making her do breathing exercises, correcting her ascending and descending tonal scales, and teaching her the rudiments of French, German and Italian. "Opera arias must be sung in the language in which they were written," she said.

Jeff was aware that I kept a journal and asked me to read it to him. He relished its flattering entries about him, and was especially amused by my caustic descriptions of Heinz Helm, whom he had not met.

Alas, one Thursday he informed me that our idyllic arrangement must be briefly interrupted; his girlfriend from Florence—an American Fulbright scholar—was coming to stay with him for the weekend. "Maybe you should go to Porto and share its sailors and soldiers with your friend Heinz?" he joked.

In fact, I was perfectly content not to see Jeff for five days, knowing that he would be there after his girlfriend's departure. Ever the diplomat, I avoided all the places where he would be sure to go with his visitor, did not show myself at Maria's and the Bar Mimi, had my dinners in trattorias in the back lanes or bought food to eat in my room. When I met Philip Dakin at the post office he, of course, knew that Jeff was temporarily otherwise occupied, and recommended me to console myself with some of the ever-available fishermen. "You know the two brothers who are always hanging around on the beach in front of my trattoria? The young one is the best-looking but still a bit shy; the older brother is better; their father is one of the best on the island, very good value; and the grandfather is a real satyr and loves it so much that he often gives another hour without charge."

But five days was not long to wait and on Monday afternoon Jeff's girlfriend left. We celebrated his freedom with a rapturous nocturnal reunion and, next day, I persuaded him to walk up into the hills with me for a picnic luncheon in a shady grove of chestnut trees among the sweet smell of myrtle bushes.

I had too long neglected Mr. Neil Little and when I went back to the Casa Meleagra, I took him one of my quaint glass bottles, that of an amply bosomed woman, possibly an Italian queen, in the hope that he would be amused by it. He was alone, and very gracious. Kurt had gone to Casamicciola to take a thermal mud bath. "At least that's what he told me," Neil said, "but I ha' me douts, as the Scots say." He led me to the new circular window on his staircase, with its view towards Mount Epomeo. "There you are, you see, I took your expert advice!" He had forgotten that I had recommended that the window should be square or oblong.

I complimented him on having been such a perfect host at his cocktail party where, like the fictional Mr. Keith in *South Wind* who had welcomed a flock of strangers who turned up because one of them had been to Easter Island, he had made me feel comfortable even without knowing that I, too, had been to Easter Island. "But you had a letter from my naughty friend Patrick," he said. "It's strange that you mention *South Wind*, because I first came to Ischia thirty years ago as a result of reading that book and have never regretted it. Now I spend all my summers here and have become a fixture and resemble that novel's Mr. Keith. Like him, my money has made me lazy, I'm afraid; but I do some thinking, and a fair lot of reading. I travel, I observe, I compare."

I told him that I envied him; it sounded like a most satisfying, indeed a perfect life, in his lovely villa with his vineyard, the sea with the long sweep of the San Francesco beach on one side and the green mountain on the other, his friends the Waltons and Herr Henze in their villas nearby, and his cheerful, charming young Kurt with him.

"Oh, that Kurt is the cross I have to bear! I often feel like murdering him. Heaven only knows why I brought him here, where every fisherman and peasant is available without complications or recriminations or tantrums! It was like taking coals to Newcastle. When this summer is over at last, I'll have to rid myself of him, buy him a bar in a Swiss ski resort, or something."

He then told me that he had devoted almost thirty years to make a comprehensive and representative collection of classic homoerotic literature, and that he was the proud possessor of choice editions of everything from the wise and uninhibited ancient Greeks and the ribald Romans of the first century A.D. to the medieval Persian poets to the volumes of Dr. Magnus Hirschfeld's researches to one of the 500 copies on special paper of the first edition of André Gide's *Corydon,* inscribed to him by the author. All these were in the library of his London house and could be openly displayed, but what he called "the real treasures of my secret life" were always with him wherever he went, now upstairs in his bedroom, to which he invited me to follow him. "Have no fear, I have no designs on your slim body, luscious as it doubtless is under that tightly fitting French sailor's *tricot.*"

His treasures were kept in a narrow box on top of his clothes cupboard, which he ceremoniously proceeded to unlock with a key that hung on a thin gold chain around his neck. The books were pornographic homosexual novels, many in paperback editions of the Olympia Press in Paris, and there were albums filled with drawings and photographs of naked boys and young men in erotic positions, singly and in couples and groups. "Do you like black boys? Arab boys? Crippled or mutilated boys? North American redskins with feather headdresses?" he asked me, turning the pages and becoming increasingly excited. "I have everything. Do you prefer them circumcised or uncut?" He had several years' issues of the American *Physique Pictorial* magazine, devoted to photographs of athletes flexing their highly developed muscles, and pointed out the cryptic signs at their bottom corners and assured me that he had been taught to interpret them. "This one means that he is bisexual, this one assumes the bottom role if paid sufficiently, this one only goes with women, more's the pity." I felt very sorry for him and left him to gloat over his sordid hoard.

On my way back to my room I met Bengt Söderberg and his friend Marc in the piazza; they were going to the Bar Mimi to sit on its terrace and watch who was arriving from Porto by the afternoon bus. They asked me to eat ice cream with them, but before we had ordered—we were given the choice of five flavors—Bengt jumped up and cried: "Quick! Let's leave and go to Maria's instead; Auden and his Jewboy are coming here and I can't bear that man's stink of sweat and piss."

We hurried along the main street and made ourselves comfortable on Maria's sidewalk viewpoint. "Poets never wash," said Marc. "Verlaine and Rimbaud were always dirty, Bertolt Brecht never washes and Jean Genet only does when he is forced to do so, in jail. What is this strange connection with great poetry and dirt?"

"That filthy Auden is not a great poet." announced Bengt. "He is only a fat, frowsy, fetid fraud."

"Now *you* are being poetical," said Marc.

They had invited Lala, Anette and Jeff and other acquaintances to visit them in the Torre Catello for light refreshments next afternoon, and now asked me to join them.

The circular Torre Catello, on a hill at the periphery of Forio and not far from my room, had been built in the ninth century to provide shelter for the people of the village during the raids of the Saracens. It consisted of a lower room arranged as a sitting room with a worktable for Bengt, with a toilet let into the immensely thick stone wall and a deep well that had supplied the besieged villagers with fresh water, and steps to the upper-floor bedroom. On one side of the tower was a trellised terrace with a dining table and a small basic kitchen; on the other side a pergola of vines ran along a vineyard. Nothing could be more romantic, exotic and delicious. Both terrace and vineyard had panoramic views over the Forio roofs and the sea. Bengt and Marc had prepared hot tea, cold fruit juices, white wine, pastries and fruit, all set out on the large table on the terrace. Among the guests were a sullen Swedish youth who planned to become that century's Lord Byron and dressed to suit the role, and a very old woman whom I had often seen in and around Forio striding along with a stout stick, a scarf over her head and wearing a long skirt, a weird, perambulating scarecrow. She was a Hungarian countess, a doctor of philosophy, fluent in eight Asiatic languages, and about to set out for China, walking there as she had done once before.

"But isn't that frightfully dangerous?" asked Lala.

"Not at all. I am an old woman, and poor. I ensure that my head and arms are covered, I wear my long skirt, and I always have a piece of needlework with me and keep my eyes demurely down on it. I am treated with great kindness and respect wherever I go. Half the time they won't even let me pay for my lodging and food."

Young Byron's eyes shone. "I wish I had the courage to do that!" he cried.

"Don't," warned the indomitable traveler. "A pretty boy like you will be robbed and raped all the way from Beirut to Peking."

Jeff, without any accompaniment, sang *Ol' Man River* and Lala permitted Anette to let us hear a brief sample of her soprano voice; but the star attraction was Bengt's and Marc's servant Nino who, after the sun had set over the sea, stripped to his white underpants and struck classical poses, his slender brown body glistening in the moonlight like an archaic Greek bronze statue awakened to life by a Pygmalion. We were all spellbound; it was a magical and unforgettable evening.

I was very happy to see more of Bengt and Marc, who shared my dislike for Mr. Auden. Being neat and tidy himself, Bengt was appalled that a famous fellow writer cared so little for his appearance. He was extremely conventional. In his highly successful novels—the first had appeared in 1948 when he was twenty-three—he took care not to be classified as a homosexual author, although those who could read between the lines understood where his own preferences lay. "Maybe I'll be bold enough in twenty years to write a gay novel," he said.*

We were of similar age and had many mutual tastes. Both of us, when we were boys, had been made to sing the words of the homoerotic Horst Wessel Song every morning before lessons began—he at a Nazi-inspired school in Sweden, I in Berlin. We both responded to the homoerotic throbbings of Wagner, Mahler and Tchaikovski. He and Marc admitted that they were as aroused as I by the daringly graphic descriptions of the sailors', dockers' and thieves' sexual antics in the novels of Jean Genet. Bengt dominated the easy-going Marc in everyday matters, but it was apparent that Marc was the more masculine, sexually commanding partner of this enviably loving pair.

And then, when I thought that my circle of Forio friends was complete, I met a blonde German beauty who became my constant and dearest daytime companion. This was Charlotte March, who made a dramatic entrance for dinner at Filippo's trattoria wearing a man's white, frilled dress shirt with gold studs, and a long billowing skirt of blue silk on which she had painted multiple-rayed smiling golden suns. Philip made a great fuss of her and introduced her to Jeff and me—"you will find her so *simpatico*," he told us—and after dinner we went with her to have coffee at Maria's, where everyone much admired her.

Her lover was Prince Heinrich von Hesse, known in Italy as Enrico d'Assio. He owned a villa at Montevergine but was staying in Capri and had installed Charlotte in an

* He did, in 1977: *A Life-Long Love*

apartment on the *piano nobile* of a large seventeenth-century palazzo, the Casa Regine by the harbor, which still retained some of its former splendors, but whose lower floors were dilapidated and had been invaded by poor Forio families. The Italian newspapers were filled that summer with revelations of scandals involving members of European nobility and expensive Italian prostitutes, and Enrico d'Assio was anxious to preserve his privacy and secretly crossed the Bay of Naples several times each week in his speedboat from Capri to visit Charlotte at night. Nobody in Forio ever saw him there.

"The sun is my symbol," she said, when Jeff and I complimented her on her skirt. "It warms the earth and makes everything grow. I am the golden girl of the sun; I worship it."

Unlike Jeff, who was happy to doze on the beach all morning and then amble from Maria's to the post office to the Bar Mimi and to Filippo's for dinner and back to his flat, Charlotte wanted to be active, to visit vineyards, to climb to the top of Mount Epomeo, to take mudbaths, to photograph everything and everyone for her fashion magazine *Die Elegante Welt*.

I welcomed the opportunity of accompanying her. Nothing sets a man off so well as having a beautiful young woman by his side. She also made another *cavaliere servante* of Kurt, whom she met at Maria's and with whom she conversed in German. My command of German had become rusty, because I seldom spoke or heard it after I left Germany as a child twenty years ago. "I am really very sorry that I was not at the Casa Meleagro last time you went there," Kurt told me. "I simply *have* to get away from there sometimes. I was at the Bar Diana in Porto, which is always a lot of fun."

Charlotte suggested that the three of us climb Mount Epomeo and spend the night at the hermitage on the summit to see the sunrise, and when Giocco heard about our plan, he proposed himself as our guide. Mr. Auden and Mr. Kallman were going to the mainland for a week, so he would be quite free, and the custodian of the hermitage was a cousin of his. "He is very ugly but a very good cook and has the biggest *cazzo* on the island," he told us.

It was a novel and pleasant experience for me not to travel alone but to have Giocco along with us to negotiate a reduced rate on the bus to Fontana, where we were to begin our hike up the mountain. When the driver called out "Serrara Fontana!" and stopped in a village, I assumed that this is where we were going and prepared to get off the bus, but Giocco made me sit down again until we reached the village of *Fontana,* without the prefix. Our ascent was exactly as George Berkeley had described his one hundred and eighty years before: "The lower parts are adorned with vines and other fruits; the middle affords pasture to flocks of goats and sheep; and the top is a sandy pointed rock, from which you have the finest prospect in the world." My Baedeker of 1887, which afforded Mount Epomeo two stars (**) and almost a full page of very small print, had become somewhat outdated in stating that "the ascent on foot is very fatiguing and should not be attempted without a guide... at the top wine and bread (1 fr.) may be obtained from the hermit, and in any case a trifling donation is expected." Since then, the road had been constructed from Fontana, and instead of a hermit there was now Giocco's cousin, the government-appointed custodian at the Hermitage to receive visitors and provide them with meals and, if required, accommodations for the night. But Herr Baedeker could not be faulted in his glowing descriptions composed for the cultured, leisured travelers of his time: "At the top are a Hermitage and the Chapel of S. Nicola, hewn in the volcanic rock. Passages and steps cut in the rock ascend to the Belvedere, commanding a strikingly beautiful panorama, embracing the bays of Gaeta and Naples. At our feet lies the island of Ischia itself; to the west the open sea; to the east the coast of Italy from Terracina, the promontory of Circello, and the Ponza islands to Capo Miseno, Vesuvius, and the Campo Campanella, the extremity of the peninsula of Sorrento; in the foreground Procida, then the indentations of the Bay of Naples, to the right the island of Capri; towards the north the distant snowy peaks of the Abruzzi."

Well, there we were, the only visitors that day. The custodian ran to greet Charlotte, Kurt and me, and embraced and kissed his cousin Giocco. His face was not merely ugly but criss-crossed with old scars that had distorted it as they healed. He was a tall, thin man with enormously large hands and feet and had a disconcerting hump on his back which did not prevent him from being extremely jovial and making jokes, most of which were apparently of a ribald nature, which Giocco attempted to translate for us. As Giocco had told us, he proved to be a very good cook and served us with a huge bowl of spaghetti, accompanied by a pungent tomato sauce with slices of sausages, garlic slivers, olives, peppers, oregano, basil leaves and dried mint. There was a salad of romaine lettuce, arugula and chicory, with olive oil and wine vinegar, and there was white and red wine, and plenty of both.

He was disappointed that neither Kurt nor I wanted to share a cell with Charlotte, and that we each preferred to have a cell for ourself, and that Giocco also wanted to be alone for the night. Each cell had two cots; two cells seemed to him to be quite adequate for four persons traveling together. Mumbling about the inconvenience and our inexplicable insistence on privacy, he nonetheless brought sheets, pillows, thin blankets and oil lamps to four cells. Then, when he had given us ample time to retire to our lonely beds, he came to each cell, opened its door and exposed himself. He was indeed endowed with a phallus of equine dimensions. "*Cazzo grande*! *Cazzo douro*!" he cried, thrusting it at Charlotte, Kurt, me and Giocco in turn. Charlotte was greatly alarmed. "*Vada via*!" she cried. I was awed but repulsed by the sight and waved him away, but Kurt and Giocco both spent some time with him.

We had told him to wake us well before sunrise, which he did by entering our cells and vigorously shaking us, without this time showing us his noble erection. We dressed and went up to the Belvedere, and the sunrise was indescribably wonderful; I had never before seen the sun appear so spectacularly and was deeply moved. "*Ja, das is ja wirklich toll*," gasped Charlotte, the sun worshipper. She was still enthralled when we sat down to breakfast. "Wouldn't it be better if there were no religions and everyone on earth worshipped the sun?" she said. "It has been worshipped since recorded time began. Why did all those other religions come and cause all the wars and fighting and controversies? Isn't it more logical to worship the sun, without which there would be no life, which gives its warmth equally to everyone on this planet."

"Wrong," said Kurt. "Not equally; it gives far too little to the Eskimos and far too much to the Negroes in Africa."

"And not enough to me in Hamburg. But we can all adapt accordingly," said Charlotte.

"What philosophers you are, and so early in the morning," I said. But I agreed with Charlotte.

The custodian expected far more than Herr Baedeker's "trifling donation" and, having received what he demanded, showed us his visitors' book and asked us to enter our names and comments in it. Charlotte, Kurt and I were overcome by laughter when we read the pompous sentiments of some of the Germans:

> *Nachdem wir früe am wolkenlosen Morgen in wenig als zwei Stunden den Epomeo erstiegen haben, belohnte uns der immergute Herrgot mit dem Ausblick über de stimmungsvolle Bucht von Neapel.*
>
> *Familie Müller, Wuppertal*
> *Korpus Kristi: Donnerstag*
> *der siebzehnte Juni,*
> *Anno Domini 1954*

Giocco advised us that, instead of returning by road to Fontana and having to wait there for the bus, it was better to make the 2-hour hike to Florio down the western slope of the mountain in the morning, while it was cool. We were somewhat doubtful of the wisdom of doing so, but followed our self-appointed guide. It had not been a good idea. There was no trail, the descent was steep and rocky, and it was by no means cool. We stumbled and fell and cut our hands when we grasped thorny bushes to steady us. Charlotte was encumbered by her camera equipment, Kurt by his powerful binoculars, I by my unwieldy map and the big architectural book and a canvas satchel containing my electric shaver and sunblock cream and insect repellent. We loudly cursed Giocco for having chosen this difficult route but he nimbly skipped ahead from rock to rock like a goat, gave forth exuberant yells of youthful joy, and jeered at our inaptitude. "E-po-meo-o is my moun-tain!" he chanted. "You are three *stu-pi-do Te-des-ci* from be-yond the Al-to A-di-ge! You are falling—you are breaking your legs—you are blee-ding all over my nice moun-tain!"

We were not amused. It was most aggravating.

When we stumbled into Santa Maria del Monte, about halfway down from the summit, we were all in a foul mood. The double door of the abandoned little church was unlocked; we entered and the pitiful state of the dim interior made us additionally dejected. Tree branches had broken in through windows and bats and birds scattered at our approach. Over the dusty altar hung a large painting of the Virgin with the infant Jesus, sitting on a puffy pink cloud, flanked by scowling angels. The canvas was badly cracked in many places.

"Is by Le-o-nar-do da Vin-ci," chanted Giocco, "a famous pain-ter of the *quin-to-cen-to* and an o-*mo*-ses-su-a-le with a *caz-zo gran-de e dou-ro!*" He was really quite impossible that morning.

We were still 1,500 feet above the sea and almost half of the island was spread out below us as on a map, every building from Forio to Lacco Ameno clearly defined. We identified Charlotte's Casa Regine by the breakwater, the Soccorso church on the promontory with its row of five black crosses, and the villas at Montevergine. Kurt trained his binoculars on the Casa Meleagro. "Don't!" I cried. "It's from a high vantage point exactly like this that the bishop in *South Wind* looked down to his cousin's villa and saw her murder her husband by pushing him over a cliff."

Kurt laughed. "Oh, I often want to murder Neil, but there is no handy cliff at the Casa Meleagro."

Somewhat rested, and in a better mood after encountering a mule track, we continued down towards Forio. On its outskirts, in Monterone, Giocco invited us into Mr. Auden's house to drink cold fruit juice, a peace offering for having offended us with his foolishness. I did not expect the poet and his lover to live in civilized surroundings but was nevertheless appalled by the filth and squalor. The house stank of greasy food and urine. There was no furniture apart from a few disintegrating canvas deckchairs. Giocco disappeared to fetch us the promised drinks.

"Who the hell are you? What are you doing here?" screeched Mr. Auden as he came awkwardly down the stairs, closely followed by Chester Kallman, and, as Giocco came out of the kitchen with a tray of glasses, "How dare you bring these people into my house, and where the hell have you been, anyway?"

Giocco remained admirably calm. "Is not your house, Signor Auden, is my aunt Angelica's house, and they are my friends," he said.

"Get rid of them!" ordered the poet.

Charlotte, Kurt and I fled.

Jeff was greatly diverted by my account of the hunchback at the Hermitage, Giocco's derisive chanting, the spurious Leonardo da Vinci painting, and our ignominious expulsion from W. H. Auden's house. "Now you know why I prefer to take it easy here," he smugly replied.

When I met Giocco at Maria's next day, he explained that Signor Auden and Signor Chester had returned earlier than expected from the mainland, and had forgiven him. Helpful as always, he went all over Forio with me to find a suitable box in which to pack my glass bottles, and a supply of wood shavings and a length of cord. At the Poste Restante desk was a note for me from Umberto di Meglio, enclosing a printed invitation card for the *End of Summer Ball* at the Grande Albergo e dei Pini, Ischia's best hotel located in a pine grove by the road to the Castello Aragonese; but as I had no formal suit with me, I offered it to Charlotte who was thrilled. "But can you go there alone?" I asked. "Oh, I won't be alone for long," she replied with perfect assurance. I went to the piazza to see her off in the bus. She wore a long dress, white and gold, white dancing shoes, white gloves to above the elbows, and a golden sun in her hair. All she needed was a wand to make her into a fairy princess.

Next morning on the beach, she gave me a full report of the evening. As soon as she arrived at the ball she was surrounded by admiring men, including Umberto di Meglio—"he asked me to give you his regards. What fabulous teeth the man has!"—and Heinz Helm who, by coincidence, was also attired in white and gold and, when they waltzed together, were presented with the prize for the best ensemble. "That Heinz is so much fun," she said. "After the ball, which was not grand at all but a small-town hop with mostly dreary local people, he took me to the Bar Diana for eggs and bacon. The place was full of sailors who, of course, were all his best friends, and he introduced me as his sister, and two of them drove me back to Forio in their jeep and were so sweet and polite."

She was so grateful to me for having given her my card that she insisted on inviting me and Jeff to dinner at her favorite pizzeria, in a small garden where the tables were arranged around a wood-fired oven from which two pizzas were pulled out at the same time and put before the owner, who then dipped his left hand into a bowl of richly flavored tomato sauce and his right hand into a bowl of grated cheese and sprinkled them over the dough. His mouth was filled with olives and he adroitly spat one onto the exact center of each pizza for the finishing touch. This performance was boisterously applauded by all the customers, mostly local people, but Jeff said he had never seen anything so disgustingly unhygienic.

Charlotte was never separated from her cameras and had taken pictures of Jeff and me on the beach, as also of Lala, Anette, Philip and Gemma and Giocco, but then she asked me to make myself available for a real "photo shoot." She wanted to produce a series of photographs of me for her magazine as a beachcomber on a small, secluded beach outside Forio where she and I would be alone. Of course I was flattered and was impressed to see a professional photographer at work, with what care and deliberation she waited patiently for the waves to crest exactly as she wanted, instructed me minutely on how to hold my head, my feet, my hands, every finger. She made me wade into the sea in my clothes and took pictures of me in my dripping blue jeans and shirt, lying half in and half out of the water as if the waves had tossed me up on the beach, and placed playing cards around me with their faces turned up, artfully arranged as if they had been scattered haphazardly, to create surrealist photographs suitable for *Die Elegante Welt.* Then she posed me with selected cards in my hand—"No, not the right, it must always be the *left*"—and always with a knave under my thumb, but not the Knave of Hearts—"he would be far too obvious!" she cried.

At the back of the beach were large boulders of tufa, and it was because of them that she had selected that beach for her work. Their rough, pitted surface appealed to her; she made me lean against one of the boulders so that its texture would contrast with my smooth, tanned face and hands and my dark, wet clothes. It all greatly perplexed me.

Both her and my stay in Ischia was now drawing to a close, and we made two more outings together, to the mud baths on the north coast and to a celebration for the gathering and pressing of the grapes at the vineyard owned by her signora of the Casa Regine.

I had not explored the north coast because the villages of Lacco Ameno and Casamicciola had been destroyed by an earthquake in 1883 and everything there was new and ugly—thermal bath establishments, an institution for the aged poor of Naples, small third-class hotels that attempted to make themselves appear superior with excrecenses in the form on "Ionic" pillars and "Gothic" turrets, a night club built in the shape of a ship. Shops sold nasty sunhats and beach baskets and examples of repulsive raffia work. Even the sanctuary of Santa Restituta, Ischia's patron saint, had been rebuilt in atrocious late-nineteenth century taste. But from hideous Casamicciola, a winding road led up to Bagni, less than half a mile away in the hills yet a tranquil world apart. Here, as in a gentle miniature central European spa, were big shady trees and pretty little thermal baths whose owners, old women dressed in the traditional black, sat crocheting outside the open doors and beckoned us to enter. It was these, not the antiseptic institutional establishments along the coast, that appealed to Charlotte and me. We looked into several of them and selected the Terme Peliazzi, undressed and submerged ourselves up to our necks in the hot, bubbling black saline-rich mud in adjoining stone troughs in which, with a certain amount of imagination, Seneca and Pliny and Petronius had lain and been cured of their arthritis twenty centuries before. After the allotted hour of this supposedly therapeutic treatment, when the matronly owner came to sluice the mud off us, and we put on our clothes, neither of us felt particularly refreshed or relaxed and an unpleasant smell continued to cling to our bodies. It had been a novel experience, but not an enjoyable one.

In Lacco Ameno, Charlotte took her last photograph of the day, of the mushroom-shaped "Il Fungo" rock in the harbor. When we returned to our dear unspoiled Forio, we overtook Jeff near Montevergine, also walking along the road.

"Goodness, what are *you* doing here? I thought you never like to leave Forio?" I asked.

He explained that he had been to the San Francesco beach as a change from our own little beach outside Filippo's. It was curious, he seemed ill at ease, almost guilty, like a naughty schoolboy who has been caught playing truant.

Charlotte's signora had told her to bring along as many friends as she wished to the party for the gathering and pressing of her grapes, but Jeff firmly declined. "You are sure to have another ghastly day. Wasn't that disaster on Mount Eopomeo enough for you?"

I was fond of him but regretted that he was so lacking in the spirit of adventure.

Philip Dakin's wife Gemma, and a number of other Forio women were going to the party; there was to be singing and dancing, and an abundance of good food. Giocco, carrying a mandolin, was escorting two young Swiss tourists who had recently arrived to enjoy the last days of summer and lauded hospitality of the local men.

The signora's vineyard produced the mountain wine that was held to be among the best in Ischia, the *Bianco superiore*, ideally suited to accompany chicken and seafood. Her vines grew on a natural platform surrounded by rugged lava crags, and, as in Norman Douglas' *South Wind*, "there was a rude structure of masonry with a vaulted chamber containing hoes and other implements of the husbandman's time-honored craft; a few chairs and a table completed the furniture." Expecting a large number of guests, Charlotte's signora and her family had provided more than a few chairs and her large table was set with many glasses and bottles of wine. Food was being cooked on a grill over a fire built on dead branches of olive trees.

When Charlotte and I arrived, greeted the signora and were introduced to various members of her family, we joined the women and children who were going to and fro through the extensive vineyard and under the trellises, picking the grapes and filling baskets with them. They carried the baskets on their heads or by their handles to empty them into three large wooden vats in which half a dozen men, young and old, in their swimtrunks or underpants, were vigorously pressing the grapes, whose juice ran along wood pipes into a large container at a lower elevation. The sweat ran down their bodies and legs to mingle with the grapes, and it was good that Jeff was not with us; he would have been deeply shocked and considered it highly unhygienic.

But Charlotte and I, eager to experience everything once, were given permission to help with the pressing. We took off our shoes, she hitched up her skirt, I rolled up my trousers and we entered one of the vats and stamped in unison with the naked men. I found it to be surprisingly difficult; the grape branches under my feet felt harder than I had anticipated. After a token participation we gave it up and joined the other guests at the table where tasty dishes now began to appear—bowls filled with large mushrooms stuffed with slices of veal and anchovies; roasted red and green peppers; the ubiquitous pasta; fish fillets sprinkled with herbs, nut kernels and Parmesan cheese, skinned and boned chicken breasts that had been cooked in a mixture of beaten eggs, breadcrumbs, black pepper and nutmeg. The men in the vats came in relays to eat, so that the stamping continued without interruption as more and more grapes were delivered. The plentitude of wine made everyone loud and animated. Giocco strummed his mandolin with fervor and sang, Gemma and the other young women danced and clapped their hands, the Swiss men and Charlotte took photographs. It was a joyful, exhilarating day, and all the more appreciated because two days later the weather changed. It became cool and cloudy and for some hours looked as if it might rain. It was the first sign that winter was not far off.

Lala hurriedly took Anette back to her well-heated house in the hills above Florence and explained that nothing was more injurious for the girl's delicate vocal cords than a sudden drop in temperature. At the Torre Catello, Bengt and Marco began packing to return to their well-heated château in Provence. I had been Signora Morena's tenant for a month, and Jeff invited me to stay in his fiat for the last week of my stay in Forio. The signora had provided me with a real home and we had a tearful farewell, but less than an hour after I had installed myself at Jeff's flat she appeared there, considerably upset, and announced that I had taken away a string of blue beads that had been lying in a bowl on the chest of drawers in my room. It was true, and I was dreadfully embarrassed and ashamed of being revealed as a thief. To gain time, I said that I did not remember taking the beads but would look through my suitcase and go back to her next morning. She trusted me to do so.

"Of course that was all nonsense about the beads," said Jeff. "She came here to check that you were really living with me, and hadn't rented another room somewhere. Italians are so weird."

Next morning I returned the beads and made the excuse that I had inadvertently packed them together with some seashells and small pieces of olive wood and tufa rock that I had collected. In fact, I had purloined the string of beads because it would be a memento of my stay, and had no value. Signora Morena took the beads into her cupped hands and kissed them and told me that she greatly treasured them because they had belonged to her mother. Then she hugged me again, and cried.

I did not see Jeff all day and when he was late for dinner at Filippo's and I was waiting for him at our regular table, Philip, who always knew what was going on in Forio, asked me if everything was alright between me and Jeff. I assured him that it was.

"Gemma and Giocco tell me that when you and Charlotte are off on your excursions, they see Jeff at Maria's and the Bar Mimi with that other Hans, the rich German who lives in a villa at Montevergine by the San Francesco beach."

Jeff had never mentioned it. When he joined me, I asked him about it.

Yes, he said, he bumped into Herr Henze occasionally at the post office and elsewhere, and was tremendously impressed that such a young man was hailed as the most important and innovative composer of the century, and was incredibly prolific, producing violin sonatas, wind quartets, piano variations, symphonies, music for ballets and operas, even recently a jazz composition. Herr Henze was most interested to have met an American Negro, a descendant of one of President Jefferson's slaves, because he was working on an opera based on Mark

Twain's *Huckleberry Finn,* in which one of the roles was that of the slave, Nigger Jim.

Our dinner was about to be set before us when a party of well-dressed people entered the trattoria and Philip, who had been informed whose yacht was anchored outside the breakwaters and who recognized who they were, hurriedly asked Jeff and me and four of his other regular customers to oblige him by giving up our tables so that he could seat them. "It is the King of Spain and his friends," he whispered to us, and offered us a complimentary meal next day.

We went away to have an inferior meal elsewhere, and later when we walked along the beach back towards Jeff's flat, we saw the king and his friends sitting on one of the breakwaters waiting for the launch from the yacht. To our surprise, His Majesty hailed us and, with the reputed politeness of kings, apologized for having usurped our table at Filippo's, asked Jeff where he was from, and then complimented me on the Royal Navy seaman's sweater I was wearing. "I like your majesty's better," I told him: it was of thin black wool, very elegant, obviously very expensive.

"So let us make an exchange," he said and pulled off his, and I slipped out of mine, having made very much the best of the bargain. The members of his entourage applauded the transaction. Their launch arrived and took them towards the lights of the royal yacht.

Then, preceded by a screaming, howling wind that rattled the windows all night, swiftly and dramatically the winter was upon us. The morning was not merely cool but quite cold. It was time to leave and to pity those who had to remain for four or five months without the blessing of the warm sun.

In northern Europe one was able to adapt oneself to the change of season. Warm clothes came out of cupboards and chests, extra blankets were put on top of beds and rubber hot-water bottles between the sheets, roast beef and mashed potatoes replaced salad meals; but in Ischia the visitors became irritable and uncomfortable. The houses were unheated and there was no place in which to escape from the cold and dampness. I almost envied the troglodytes who could retreat with their animals into their caves. The Casa Meleagra was closed, locked and shuttered. W. H. Auden and Chester Kallman disappeared overnight, leaving behind them a shattered house and owing Giocco two months' wages, as well as unpaid bills at the baker, the butcher, the grocer, the wine merchant and the Bar Mimi. Charlotte heard from Heinz Helm that he was going to spend the winter in a village in Algeria, near the barracks of the French Foreign Legion.

On Jeff's and my last day together, he told me that he could not have dinner with me because Herr Henze had invited him to his villa. The leading role of the new opera based on *Huckleberry Finn*, that of the slave, Nigger Jim, who is the tale's real hero, would ideally suit Jeff's appearance and voice, and he was anxious to discuss it further with Jeff.

"Imagine what it will mean for me if I play my cards right tonight," he told me—he meant, if he performed in bed like the proverbial big black American stud. "I'll be launched on a great international operatic career!"

I wished him all possible success and went sadly to spend my last evening at Filippo's alone. I did not blame Jeff for abandoning me, but was hurt by it, and then regretted that our liaison had prevented me from supporting the local fishermen's main industry by never in five weeks having availed myself of their sexual favors. I finished my solitary meal, paid for it, and bade Philip a fond and almost tearful farewell. The fishermen brothers of whose good qualities, as of those of their father and grandfather, Philip had so graphically told me, were as usual still idling by their boats drawn up on the beach, ready to be hired for an hour's fishing trip. Being tossed about on the sea in the dark in a small sailboat did not appeal to me, but I sauntered across to the brothers, stood close to them and forced myself to leer insinuatingly and boldly jiggled the coins in my trouser pocket. I then walked away up the steps into the piazza and, having looked back and seen the younger of the brothers negligently follow me, walked to the nearby house in which Jeff had his flat, and to the outside stairs leading to it—but by the time I had reached the bottom of the steps and went up and unlocked the door of the flat, I became increasingly uncomfortable with the situation I had created. I felt foolish and sordid but did not know how to politely dismiss the surly youth who now stood provocatively posed facing me in Jeff's room. Then I had an inspiration: the box with my remaining five bottles stood on the floor, the length of cord beside it, because I was waiting for Jeff to help me by pulling the cord while I secured it tight around the box. I showed the fisherman what had to be done, and the "gorgeous young men's muscles," which Faith Jaques had extolled so highly, were put to good use. The box was firmly corded, I pressed a generous tip into the fisherman's hand and he left. I was enormously relieved and went to bed to await Jeff's return.

Next morning—it was Sunday, October 1—Jeff and I, with all our luggage, boarded the bus to Porto, which conveniently connected with the ferryboat to Naples.

It had been a wonderful summer, with five weeks of perfection in Forio for the equivalent of two dollars a day—one for my room, and one for three daily meals. Five weeks without the curse of television, radio, amplified so-called music, telephone and English language newspapers to detract from the tranquil, blissful days and nights. And, in addition to having a glorious time, my stay in Ischia had been unexpectedly productive, because I would write a book about it. I did not know if it would be a factual travel account with comic interludes in the manner of the eccentric and perceptive Robert Byron's *The Road to Oxiana*, with photographs by Charlotte March, or a novel like Norman Douglas' *South Wind*, with characters modeled on the local people and summer residents I had met, and incorporating dissertations on the island topography, history, viniculture and architecture. For either enterprise, my annotated map and book of the island's buildings would be invaluable to me. I would dedicate the book to Jefferson Jordan and its title would be *The Ithyphallic Hunchback of Mount Epomeo*.

— 3 —

A Mediterranean Cruise

Until I moved to New York, I was for many years the cruise director for the Society for Hellenic Travel in England and my two most memorable cruises were to the Black Sea and Russia, about which I have written in an earlier book,* and in September of 1956 a cruise around the Mediterranean, on which the eighty-year-old Professor John Garstang was the *Guest of Honour.*

Professor Garstang, C.B.E.—he had been made a Companion of the British Empire by the King of England in acknowledgement of his many archaeological achievements—was born in 1876 and first investigated Hittite sites in southern Turkey in 1890. Early in the twentieth century, he conducted excavations at Abydos in Egypt, Meroë in the Sudan, and in Jericho, Palestine; but the continuing

* *Volleyball with the Cuna Indians, and Other Gay Travel Adventures,* Viking Penguin, 1993.

search for knowledge about the little-known Hittite civilization in Cilicia remained his chief interest and passion, and his excavation of a Hittite tel—an artificial mound—near Mersin in the 1920s was his greatest triumph.

The Society for Hellenic Travel provided four lecturers for the cruise to give talks during the days at sea and provide expert guidance at the sites ashore, and had, in addition, invited Professor Garstang because the cruise itinerary included a call at Mersin, where he would be able after fifty years to revisit the tel that had gained him his greatest fame.

He was accompanied by his sister, Mrs. Gurney, and her son. His sister had married well—the Gurneys are an old and highly respected banking family from Norwich, and people in England who have never heard of Croesus say of someone who is exceedingly rich that he is "as rich as a Gurney." A trained nurse traveled with him and shared a cabin with Mrs. Emily Villiers-Stuart, his aristocratic secretary. He was so frail that, when I first saw him being led along the platform at London's Victoria Station, I thought he would not survive the train journey to Venice. When he did arrive aboard the SS *Proleterka,* he kept to his cabin in order to conserve what little energy he could still summon for the visit to the famous tel at Mersin.

Before the ship sailed, some of the passengers strolled into St. Marks's Square and returned on board wearing gondoliers' hats with bright red ribbons. The lecturers were indignant. "How positively *ghastly*—so utterly vulgar. Is this a meaningful Hellenic cruise or a cheap pleasure trip?"

cried Professor A. R. Burn of Oxford University. "Come away, A. R., and let's go over the notes of your first lecture," his prim, shrewish wife told him.

The *SS Proleterka*, a Jugoslav ship that had been chartered for the cruise, was run in true proletarian manner for the benefit of its crew, not the passengers. Loud jazz music, intensely offensive to the scholarly travelers, blared on decks and throughout the public rooms, and the deck chairs were occupied by burly members of the engine room crew. When I remonstrated with the purser, he swept aside my complaints. "The men in the engine room work very hard; it is very hot down there. They deserve to have some fresh air and sun. And they like the music."

"But the passengers—"

"Say me nothing about the passengers. They are of no importance to us; we will never see them again. Our crew stay with us for many years and must be made happy."

I asked him whether the crew expected the passengers to take up a contribution for them at the end of the cruise.

"Of course. That is taken for granted."

"Well," I told him, "unless you turn off the jazz music except when the passengers are ashore, and unless all the deckchairs are kept for the use of the passengers, there will be no contribution, no tips."

He was furious, but ten minutes later the music stopped and the engine room crew vacated the decks.

In London I had recruited Dr. Harry Young to travel with us as *Accompanying Physician.* He was good-looking and had had brief affairs or one-night-stands with half a dozen of my friends, who spoke highly of his bedside manner. I had hoped that he would be a congenial companion for me during the cruise, but he studiously avoided me and devoted his time and turned on his charm to all the unattached women passengers, regardless of their age, and assiduously danced with them in the saloon after dinner.

The shore excursions at Trogir and Kotor on the Jugoslav coast were uneventful. In Athens, the obnoxious Professor Burn showed his teeth. The ship lay alongside the quay in the port of Piraeus and was scheduled to sail at midnight for Bodrum in Turkey, where the remains of the Dorian city of Halicarnassus were to be explored. At dinner on board, when I announced that, as the *SS Proleterka* would depart at midnight, some of the passengers might like to go into Piraeus where there were lively tavernas with bazouki music, Professor Burn jumped up, took a commanding position in the center of the dining room and, with his face made hideous by anger, shouted, "Instead of getting us out of here and on our way to have ample time tomorrow for the mausoleum of Halicarnassus, one of the seven wonders of the ancient world, our Cruise Mis-director appears to want us to waste our time in some ghastly, stinking nightclub whose proprietor no doubt pays him commission!"

He had gone too far; it was slander, and Mary Gough, the wife of Professor Michael Gough, also an Oxonian scholar, loudly said, "It takes this ship only eight hours to get from here to Bodrum; we will be there by eight tomorrow morning and have plenty of time. Meanwhile, I vote for the tavernas." I felt like giving her a big hug.

We did indeed have plenty of time next day in Bodrum, not only to inspect the site of the mausoleum, of which only its foundation stones remained, buried in the grassy hill, but also to walk through the massive crusader castle of St. Peter. When we returned to the port, our Dr. Young came out of the police station appearing strangely embarrassed. "They heard that I am a doctor, and some of the men asked me for my professional assistance," he explained.

Mrs. Gough was walking beside me. "Oh, everyone who has read Lawrence's *Seven Pillars of Wisdom* knows all about Turkish policemen," she said.

I had been to Rhodes four times and never admired the castle of the Knights of St. John, which the Italians, during their occupation of the island between 1912 and 1947, have so monstrously over-restored; nor did I consider it necessary to go on the motorcoach excursion to ancient Lindos, which was accompanied by our four lecturers, all of whom planned to address "a few words" of explanation to the passengers, although Professor Burn had stated that he, being the authority on the place, could very well do so without his learned colleagues' support. Instead, I decided to go to the beach for some rest and relaxation from my duties, and was astonished when Dr. Young told me that he would join me. "I'm glad you're coming with me, but surprised; you've avoided me all week," I told him.

"Hanns, surely you understand why! As a doctor I must be very careful always to keep up proper appearances. If I'm seen too much with you the passengers might suspect that I'm also a queer; and that would be the end of my professional career."

We arrived at Mersin on September 11 and the *SS Proleterka* anchored out in the bay, a mile from the town. After breakfast, the passengers and the lecturers were taken ashore by caiques. Several buses were waiting on the quay to take them on a long excursion to Kiz Kalesi, the Byzantine "Maiden's Castle" near Silifke, and to the caves of Heaven and Hell and Kanlidivane, an early Greek site with a necropolis, where they were to have a picnic luncheon in the shade of trees. In the afternoon, they would drive back toward Mersin and at 4.30 P.M., when it was a little less hot, stop at the famous Hittite tel where Professor Garstang would greet them and hopefully be able to say a few words, and Professor Michael Gough would give an explanatory talk.

As soon as the last contingent of passengers had left the ship, the loudspeakers as usual blared forth the throbbing, pulsating jazz that was the crew's delight. Professor Garstang, his sister and his nurse had remained on board and I knew that they hated this so-called music as much as I did, but I could not be bothered yet again to plead with the unobliging purser to have it turned off, or at least lowered in volume.

Near us, a German freighter was anchored; it was empty and looked top-heavy, riding high in the filthy, ochre waters of the bay. Its sailors sat in rows on the rails, presenting their bare backs to us, and their radio also blared out loud dance music. Between the ships, greasy barrels, disintegrating packing cases and kitchen refuse floated about. Mersin was a blur in the sun and, after the departure of the fleet of tourist buses, appeared to be deserted.

The plan for the day was that, at twelve noon precisely, Professor Garstang was to be taken ashore, where his old friend Mr. Aptulla Kuran, the owner of the Mersin Hotel, would provide luncheon and drive him to the tel in good time to meet the cruise passengers there at 4:30 P.M. I offered to go into town early in the morning to contact Mr. Kuran and make the arrangements, but Mrs. Villiers-Stuart played the role of secretary to the full and told me in no uncertain terms that my services were not required and went off with the other passengers to attend to everything personally. "We do not want there to be a muddle about this; it is a great day for the professor," she said. She would send a caique back to the *SS Proleterka* at noon to take the professor and his sister and the nurse ashore.

This was the plan. All morning the professor kept to his bed while his sister fussily ran from her cabin to his and back again, giving the nurse unnecessary instructions, and assembling parasols, a pneumatic cushion, and thermos jugs of boiled, iced water.

Some of the crew, notwithstanding the dirt of the water in the bay, dived into the sea and splashed about like happy schoolboys, screaming and shouting. None were permitted to go ashore except one steward who was to assist the professor; the others envied him as he washed and ironed his uniform.

At eleven o'clock, the nurse began to dress the professor and shortly before noon she appeared on deck, supporting him and walking very slowly beside him. He wore a pale gray linen suit, much too large and loose for his emaciated body, and a white shirt with the tie of the Society of Antiquaries. The shirt, too, was too large for him and its collar hung low around the base of his thin neck. He had a green celluloid sun visor, worn under his floppy white hat to protect his eyes, and the nurse had placed a neatly folded handkerchief in the breast pocket of his jacket.

Mrs. Gurney twittered excitedly at her brother's appearance on deck. "John, darling!" she cried, running up to him. "You are back again! Look—" and she pointed across the bay to the town. "Mersin again, John! Aren't you happy?"

But I looked towards the town with trepidation, for there was no sign of the boat which Mrs. Villiers-Stuart had promised to send out to the ship. Mrs. Gurney and the nurse made the professor comfortable in a chair and we waited, but when, after twenty minutes, no caique had yet detached itself from the quay, I went to the purser's office. The professor was already becoming impatient and irritable. "When are we going ashore?" he grumbled. "I want my lunch. I don't want to keep my friend Aptulla Kuran waiting."

"Don't worry, John," Mrs. Gurney assured him. "Emmy has it all arranged." She and the nurse had implicit faith in the professor's secretary, but I was less certain of her capabilities.

"How can we get in touch with the shore?" I asked the purser. "It is urgent. We must get a boat to come out."

He said that the agreed signal was three blasts on the ship's siren, and presently three deep blasts sounded across the water and were after some minutes repeated in acknowledgment from the port. Then something did at last move along the quay, a dark shape moved away from it and became a caique, which made its way in an arc towards the *SS Proleterka*.

"The boat is coming, John! Here comes Emmy's boat!" cried Mrs. Gurney. "Oh, where is the steward, and where are the professor's pills, nurse? And where is his air cushion?"

The big moment had arrived and I did not underestimate the difficulties that might lie ahead that afternoon. "Come along now, my darling," the nurse encouraged her patient, helping him out of the chair and putting his stick into his hands. The steward arrived, a big, blond fellow, freshly shaved and handsome in his starched white uniform, and I supervised the crew who lowered the gangway into the best possible position. The caique, manned by two tough Turks and a surprisingly fair-haired boy, tossed up and down on the waves and was joined to the *SS Proleterka* only by one boatman, who stood with one of his bare feet in the caique and the other hooked under the bottom step of the gangway. He swayed rhythmically as his knees bent and straightened in turn.

Mrs. Gurney descended first, then the nurse who handed the professor to me and the steward. Slowly, step by step, she walked backwards down the gangway so that she faced her patient and gently coaxed him to come to her: "Come on, my darling—that's right—you can't fall, darling."

"No, I can't fall," said Professor Garstang.

When the steward and I had brought him to the bottom of the gangway, he hung there between us and saw the anxious faces of his sister and his nurse in the unstable caique. The boatmen shouted and beckoned; one of them grabbed the helpless old man around the waist and, as Mrs. Gurney screamed in fear, he partly pulled and partly pushed Professor Garstang into the arms of his sister and the nurse. His hat had blown away but was retrieved and set back on his head, and this minor mishap relieved the tension and gave Mrs. Gurney the opportunity to laugh as the boatmen began to row for the shore. "Fancy, John: almost lost your hat!" she cried merrily, and then, "Look, John—Mersin!"

She had never been to the site of her brother's greatest triumph but its name was dear to her and embued with romance, success and lauded achievement. She had heard him speak of the tel at Mersin for so many decades and felt that this day was for her, too, a homecoming.

"I want my lunch," said the professor.

"And you shall have it, Emmy will be at the harbor with a carriage for us"—and so she was, standing on the concrete quay with tears in her eyes.

It was less difficult to transfer the professor from the caique to the quay than I had feared, and when he stood on *terra firma,* held up between the steward and me, the women fluttered around him and pecked his pale cheeks and congratulated him.

"Welcome back to Mersin!" cried Mrs. Villiers-Stuart.

"Oh, John, you're really here!" cried Mrs. Gurney. "But where is Aptulla?" asked the professor. It was almost two o'clock and he was hungry.

"I have two carriages waiting for us just outside the port gate," explained Mrs. Villiers-Stuart, eager to be praised for the arrangements she had made and offering no explanation for having failed to send a caique for us at noon. "Two adorable old carriages with horses with pink feathers on their heads."

The steward and I walked the professor along the quay, through the deep shade of the port gate and into the dazzle of a small, dusty square where, at the sight of the waiting carriages, the women broke into exclamations of delight. While Mrs. Gurney patted the diseased-looking horses and regretted that she had brought them no cubes of sugar from the ship, none could decide in which carriage she would travel, or with whom, or who would sit with the professor. "We really must get going," I suggested as they continued to dither by the carriages, and although the sister and the secretary made it clear that they disliked criticism of their arrangements and preferred to take their own time, they ordered the professor to be placed in the first carriage between them. "To the hotel!" they gaily called to the driver, and left the nurse, the steward and me to follow in the other carriage.

The progress of the carriages was exasperatingly slow as they clattered through ever narrower lanes between wagons, loaded high with farm produce, and ancient motorcars. The Mersin Hotel was apparently located at a very considerable distance from the port and I became certain that the drivers must have misunderstood. "To Mersin Oteli! Mersin Oteli!" I called out. The drivers nodded.

After a while the carriages turned sharply to the left, and then left again, and presently the roads widened and the houses on either side were larger. We passed a market, where everyone looked up to see the cavalcade pass, and drew up before a forbidding, dun-colored building. The drivers demanded to be paid.

We all descended, glad at last to have arrived. Not inclined to bargain and being unfamiliar with the Turkish currency, I paid colossal amounts. The drivers smirked, winked at each other, whipped up their thin old horses and drove away.

A sign over the doorway showed that we had not been taken to a wrong place. This was the Mersin Oteli. A steep flight of stairs led directly from the street to the second floor. The steward and I made a cat's cradle of our arms and carried up the professor, who showed himself to be well pleased with this novel means of transportation. The women followed us.

Upstairs, the desk, with its ornate mahogany and empty mailboxes behind it, was unguarded. No one appeared at the sound of the little brass bell. The professor hung like a rag doll between the steward and me while the nurse patted his face lightly to bring some blood into it, but his eyelids drooped. He was exhausted by the effort of having been taken ashore, and more than half-asleep from lack of food. We carried him along a dark corridor in which the heavily embossed and richly gilt wallpaper had peeled off in wide, hanging strips. The doors on both sides had panels painted purple, green and sickly red and yellow. We opened a door at random, found the room to be unoccupied, and laid Professor Garstang on one of the four beds. The nurse fussed over him and while the sister and secretary opened wide the window and deposited their bags, satchels, cameras, hats, parasols and the air cushion and thermos flasks on tables and chairs, I went to explore the hotel and to find Mr. Kuran. The steward sat on a bench in the corridor, wiped his sweaty face and lit a cigarette.

I could not find Mr. Kuran, or anyone else. All the rooms that were not locked were empty, and so was a windowless space with a stove and a sink, neither of which seemed to have been used for years. The sounds of my ringing the bell and calling out "Mr. Kuran! Mr. Kuran!" echoed along the corridor. Only the absence of some keys from the board behind the desk bore witness to the fact that more than ghosts inhabited the Mersin Oteli.

There were footsteps coming up the stairs, and a ragged urchin appeared, about fourteen years old and evidently in charge of the establishment.

"Where is Mr. Kuran?" I demanded of him. "*Dove* Signor Kuran? *Ou est* Monsieur Kuran?" The boy stared at me idiotically. Flies clustered in the corners of his eyes.

"Monsieur Kuran!" I cried, like the tourist who believes that, by shouting, he can make the stupid foreigner understand.

The boy gave no visible sign of comprehension but picked up the archaic telephone, click-clicked with a dirty finger and shouted to someone at the other end, released the receiver and gave me to understand that Mr. Kuran was coming.

This at least brought hope, and I returned to the others.

The professor had dozed off and his women sat in a semi-circle facing the window, through which the sea could be seen; and less than a stone's throw away to the left was the quay where we had arrived and the gate through which we had passed to the carriages.

"Oh! And they drove us for *miles*!" I cried.

The women, having already discovered the deception, were smug. "Yes, in a circle; the old trick," said Mrs. Gurney. They gazed wistfully across the bay to the *SS Proleterka,* a sleek haven of civilization and comforts, looking very white and fine in comparison to the ugly German freighter.

"Where is Mr. Kuran?" asked Mrs. Villiers-Stuart.

"Coming, I hope," I said.

"We all hope so," said Mrs. Gurney pointedly.

"But didn't you tell him that we were coming?" I asked Mrs. Villiers- Stuart. "You did say you were going to arrange it all."

"Well," she defended herself, "I was led to understand that it *had* all been arranged and that I only had to get the carriages. And I did get the carriages."

"It is usually you who makes the shore arrangements," said Mrs. Gurney. "This muddle is extremely unfortunate. It is getting on for three o'clock and we have had no luncheon."

When we arrived at the hotel I had noticed a pastry shop next door. I ran down to it, had a large paper bag filled with assorted dry biscuits, took it up to the room and offered it to the professor and his women; but instead of being grateful to me, they refused to take any. "No," decreed Mrs. Gurney, speaking for them all. "We have no intention of spoiling our appetite for luncheon."

"Well, I hope you'll get some," I told her, greedily eating biscuits.

"Oh yes, we are lunching with the professor's old friend, Mr. Kuran," said Mrs. Gurney complacently.

The boy with the flies around his eyes ran towards us and beckoned to me to follow him to the reception desk. A stout, elderly, unshaven and irritated man was climbing up the stairs. He wore khaki trousers, wrinkled and spotty, and a pale green shirt open at the neck.

"Are you Mr. Kuran?" I cried eagerly. The man, neither admitting nor denying it, said, "Why have you brought Greek ladies to my hotel?"

"I have brought you Professor Garstang," I said, with as much dignity I could muster.

Instantly, Mr. Kuran was no longer irritated at having had his afternoon nap disturbed. He was both aghast at the information and delighted.

"Professor Garstang!" he cried, peering along the dark corridor and starting to move forward. "My old friend the professor is in my hotel after all these years! But why was I not told of this?"

"But I thought his secretary—" I began, and then gave it up. What did it matter. Now everything would go according to plan. "We went into one of the empty room," I explained. "I hope that was alright."

"Greeks, I was told! Greeks come on the ship today," cried Mr. Kuran. "*Greeks*! It is terrible." He bounded with agility up to the professor and, unaware that the old man was asleep, took hold of his hands and shook them wildly. "Oh, my dear old friend!" he cried.

The woman all started to their feet and the professor shook himself awake like a child. He blinked weakly with startled, terrified eyes as he saw the man bending over him who pressed his ruddy, bloated face to his and kissed him upon both cheeks. "Nurse!" he whimpered, making no effort to repulse the onslaught.

Mr. Kuran desisted; the nurse patted and soothed her patient. "We are in Mersin, my darling, at the hotel, and here is your old friend Mr. Kuran."

"Ah, Aptulla," sighed the professor, comprehending now and stretching out a hand to his friend. *"Avez vous jamais pense a me revoir, cher ami?"*

Mr. Kuran was weeping. *"Mais oui, mais oui!"* he cried.

"The professor is very hungry," announced Mrs. Gurney, "and so are we all. And at four-thirty we are due at the professor's tel, to meet the cruise passengers."

"*Quelle horreur*! The professor's tel is far away, but we will go in my new American car, the professor and some of you good ladies, and a friend of mine will take the others. I am at your disposal. But why was I not told? Greeks, they said."

"And luncheon?" asked Mrs. Gurney.

I hoped that there would be none, so that she would regret to her dying day having refused my thoughtful offer of the biscuits, but Mr. Kuran hurried away to have some food brought to us. "I give no longer food in my hotel, like in the time when the professor and Mrs. Garstang were here, but I go now to have chicken and rice sent across."

"Dear Mr. Kuran has gone to get us our luncheon, John," Mrs. Gurney assured her famished brother. "It won't be long now. Chicken and rice, we're to have. You'll like that, won't you?"

We waited. The nurse fanned her patient's face and gave him some of the boiled, iced water. The ship's steward in the corridor had gratefully accepted my biscuits and sat leaning against the wall. He had smoked his last cigarette and I had none to give him, nor did I feel obligated to go back into the street and buy some for him. It was very hot. Three quarters of an hour later, Mr. Kuran returned and brought with him three men who carried plates of chicken legs and sodden rice.

Mr. Kuran's new American car was very splendid, cyclamen pink, and amazingly long, and adorned with many chromium decorations, but proved to be extremely difficult for the professor to enter. Its doors were made either for dwarfs or men possessed of rubber bones. It would have been far easier to place the professor in the car of Mr. Kuran's friend, which was less spectacular and had no green windscreen and side windows but, being older and more roomy, made access and egress effortless; but Mr. Kuran insisted that he must have the honor of driving the professor to his tel and contrived to make him sit beside him in the front seat. In order to be on hand to help him to get out of the car, the steward and I and the nurse sat in the back seat. We were late, and the two cars raced each other, hooting and throwing up clouds of dust, so that Mrs. Gurney and Mrs. Villiers-Stuart in the slower car feared they would become sick and throw up the greasy meal that they had hurriedly gulped down.

We crossed a dry river by an iron bridge, which swayed as the cars dashed over it, and then there were no more houses, fences, overhead electricity or telephone lines. We drove between undulating sandy, rocky dunes that resembled huge ochre waves and stretched right and left as far we could see. "Is it much further?" I asked, anxiously, watching the professor being thrown alternatively against the Mr. Kuran and the car window. "No. We are arrived," said Mr. Kuran.

He stopped the car and even I, having been warned that the famous tel would be a most disappointing sight, looked in vain for any Hittite foundations, grave stones, walls, fallen columns. We seemed to be in the middle of nowhere. The motorcoaches with the cruise passengers had not arrived. The second car came along the rough track toward us and stopped beside Mr. Kuran's car. "Do you remember the place, my dear old friend?" he asked the professor, pointing.

"No, dear Aptulla," said Professor Garstang. With the nurse's help the steward and I managed to extricate him from the car. We put him on his feet and set his hat back on his head.

The artificial hill was higher than the surrounding natural ones and steeper, partly covered by loose stones and rocks as a result of the excavations. It was quite bare and exposed to the relentless sun. High up, one segment of the hill had been cut away; its soil and rubble had been sifted and meticulously examined, but this had been done half a century before and, after having been totally abandoned for the past twenty years or more, all that now remained of the famous tel was a curiously eroded mound.

Mrs. Gurney and Mrs. Villiers-Stuart put up their parasols and stumbled to and fro across the stony ground at the bottom of the tel. "We must find some shade for the professor," they told me. "Where is he to sit? Perhaps he should have stayed in that hideous vulgar car. Where are the others, Mr. Ebensten? Didn't you tell them to meet us here at four-thirty? It is almost five, now."

But the professor softly said: "I must go to the top of the tel. Carry me up, my two strong young men." The steward and I again clasped hands and sat the old man on the seat thus formed. The nurse took his stick and carefully made her way up the hill behind us.

Mrs. Gurney and Mrs. Villiers-Stuart gesticulated, stretched out useless hands and called out directions: "Up this way—bring him this way—no, round here—let him sit down there—no, not as high as that—oh, if only there were a bit of shade for him—carry him that way—" and the professor, hanging between the steward and me, began silently to cry with emotion. As the tears ran down his nose and cheeks, he whimpered, "I have made it, nurse; you said I should not try to make it, but I am here."

The steward understood no English, but I was deeply moved: it was not the sweat of my exertions that clouded my eyes. Ignoring the conflicting suggestions of the women, we stopped before an unusually large boulder just below the top of the mound, which cast a very narrow strip of shade along its base, and there we lowered the old man to the ground. The nurse slipped the pneumatic cushion under him and sat beside him to help shelter him from the sun.

We had arrived—but where were the passengers and the lecturers who should have been there half an hour before? The heat was vicious in this wilderness. We waited. The steward, having been given a cigarette by Mr. Kuran, smoked and looked down at the parked cars and surely wondered why we had come to that god-forsaken place and how long he had to stay there with us. The professor grumbled softly about the heat, asked why the others were not there, and complained that the stones on which he lay hurt him, despite the air cushion. Seeing him become increasingly impatient and exhausted, the nurse gave him iced water to sip and petted him and prattled into his ear, calling him her darling and telling him how proud he must feel to have realized his great wish.

I idly searched among the rocks and rubble until I found some reddish potsherds half exposed in the dry soil. None was large but I extracted a few of them and took the largest to the professor. It was quite plain and insignificant, just a piece of broken pottery, and I neither knew nor cared if it was Hittite or had been dropped there only a month before; but it would serve my purpose. "Look what I have found!" I said brightly, showing my find to the professor.

"What is it?"

Professor Garstang held out a hand, took the potsherd and closed his thin, crab-like fingers around it. He said nothing, but gently transferred my find to his jacket pocket, pushing it down behind the handkerchief that the nurse had placed there. It was his; like every object discovered there fifty years before by his teams of bustling hired laborers, it had been brought to him and become his, part of his life's work, to be examined at leisure and studied and measured and photographed and catalogued and drawn to scale, tagged and packed and finally stored upon a shelf behind glass at his command. It was his; and I regretted the loss with a strange, biting intensity, wounded at being deprived of this fragment of worthless pottery and hurt not even to be praised for having found it.

"Here they are at last!" called out Mrs. Villiers-Stuart, who stood like a chamois on a rock a little higher than the others.

It was true. Two motorcoaches had arrived at the base of the tel and two others were advancing shakily along the track, each with a cloud of dust in its wake. Accompanied by many small boys who had ridden on the roofs of the coaches, the passengers of the *SS Proleterka* ascended the tel like an attacking army of gaudily-shirted and floral-skirted, be-hatted and sun-goggled insects. They were laughing, despite the heat on that fatiguing day, and longing to tell us why they were late and what adventures had befallen them at Kiz Kalesi and in the Cave of Hell. But as they reached the top of the mound, they advanced slowly, as to an altar in a church, and grouped themselves silently in acute embarrassment, not knowing where to look; for they were confronted by a terrible sight in that terrible place—a gray, awry puppet half slumped on the rough ground and half reclining against the crouching nurse, its arms dangling limp, its head tilted back with vacant eyes peering out from under the ugly green visor, an ancient doll flung down in the wilderness and guarded, as if by sinister sentinels, by the heat-dazed women and the distraught Cruise Director.

They were struck dumb, but the shuffling of all those many pairs of feet made a continuous, crunching noise as they stood in a circle, at a respectful distance, around the professor; and when they were all there—the local boys sitting before them or on rocks high above, the four bus drivers at the back, craning their necks, and Mr. Kuran and his friend looking on benignly—Professor Michael Gough stepped forward. Much to the chagrin of the insolent Professor Burn, the other lecturers had chosen him to address us there.

"Ladies and gentlemen," he said, "we have come here not because there is now a great deal to see, but in order to make a pilgrimage. The site before you is famous not for any beauty, but for the knowledge which it has yielded. I shall not keep you here long, for we have all had a long, busy, rewarding day. It is enough that we now end it by seeing the place to which Professor John Garstang first came fifty years ago and from which he extracted the evidence that has caused us completely to rewrite the Hittite chapters in our history books. Here, he patiently and scientifically searched this artificial mound or tel, as we call it, and his findings taught him so much about the people who lived here more than two thousand years before the coming of Christ—and I must remind you that when Professor Garstang first began his excavation, he had great difficulty in obtaining permission from the local Pasha to dig and remove his finds. What you see here now must not disappoint but thrill you, for you see the bare fabric that has given up the secrets of an ancient civilization."

He stopped, with bowed head, and the many pairs of feet shuffled; and then we heard another man's voice, which only very few of those present had heard before, an actor's voice, rich and ripe, that demanded attention and earned respect. It was the voice of Professor Garstang, who had somehow raised himself to a sitting position, with the nurse kneeling behind him and supporting his back.

"Ladies and gentlemen," he said slowly, staring before him and emphasizing each word: "What you see here is the ruin of a site, and the wreck of a man."

And, having made this dramatic effort, the old man slumped back into his nurse's arms and, at a sign from her, the steward and I raised him up and as he hung for a moment between us with his knees bent and only the tips of his shoes touching the ground, the passengers raised their cameras and trained them upon him to record a memorable scene that would look well in their albums.

"What is happening?" asked the professor, unable to see clearly in the dazzling light of the sun, now very low in the sky. "You are being photographed," I told him.

"In color, or only in the old black-and-white?" he asked impishly, and I said: "In both, and even in moving pictures."

"I hope someone will send a picture to dear old auntie *Times*," he said. Archaeologists, like actors long forgotten by their fans and *prima donnas* past their prime, continue to their last days to crave favorable press publicity.

Then the steward and I carried the old man down his mound as fast as we could, with the nurse hurrying along beside us, and there was a great noise suddenly, a fearful swooping in the air above us, but neither the steward nor I could look up to see what caused it, and it passed over us. But the cruise passengers and lecturers on the tel stood enthralled, looking up and aiming their cameras on the huge flock of Cilician storks, which were migrating to Africa for the winter.

Mr. Kuran had a brandy flask in his car and offered it to the professor, who took a few sips while the nurse held it for him. "The sooner he gets back to the ship the better," she said.

We drove away but after having crossed the bridge over the dry river and reached the first houses of Mersin, instead of making for the port, Mr. Kuran turned the car inland. "Where are you taking us?" I cried in alarm, and, when he did not answer me, I added emphatically: "We must get the professor back to the ship without delay!"

Mr. Kuran muttered something about taking only a few minutes. We were in his hands and had no alternative but to trust him. He drove past some orchards to where modern houses built of concrete, each like an assortment of boxes stacked up together, stood in gardens with flowerbeds in geometric patterns. He stopped outside one of these horrors and loudly sounded the car horn. "It is my house," he proudly explained.

"But we really must get back to the ship," I said, and the nurse nodded in agreement.

"Only one minute!" called out Mr. Kuran, as he ran into his garden and around his house, calling for his wife. We saw her for a moment. Then, as he told her the reason for his visit, she went quickly back into the house.

We turned down all the windows of the car to make it less hot. Every minute that passed seemed like an hour, and I was about to run into the house and demand that Mr. Kuran drive us back to the port immediately, when he reappeared with his wife beside him. She was a large, apricot-colored woman with sleek black hair. The delay had been caused by her having changed her clothes; to receive us in proper style, she now wore a magnificent long dress of glistening blue brocade shot with gold, high-heeled shoes, and a considerable amount of flashy gold jewelry. Like a salesman producing his most priced object, Mr. Kuran led her up to the professor. She stooped to look through the car window and a plump arm, heavy with gold bracelets, insinuated itself like a snake into the

Cadillac. The ringed fingers searched for the old man's hand.

"This is my wife, Professor Garstang," said Mr. Kuran.

"Ah, vous avez bien de la chance, cher Aptulla," said the professor. *"Et vous, madame, vous êtes bien belle."*

Mr. Kuran flashed a proud smile. "And now we can go," he said.

"Au revoir, au revoir!" called out his wife, and, glad to be on our way at last, we all waved back to her as the car turned wildly in the road, almost knocking down the ornate iron fence, and then headed for the port.

"My wife would never have forgiven me," said Mr. Kuran, "if I come to her tonight and tell her that my old professor has been here and I did not present her to him."

In Mersin, we saw the four dusty buses parked in the main square. The passengers were negotiating for the purchase of carpets and brassware and risking their health by eating the ice-cream and sherbert pressed on them by squalid street vendors.

The wind, which always blows in from the sea at sundown in Mersin, made the assembled caiques in the harbor toss about mightily on the water. Mrs. Gurney and Mrs. Villiers-Stuart, having arrived at the port long before us in the car of Mr. Kuran's friend and being in a state of nerves about our delay, looked with dismay at the choppy sea that swept over the concrete quay. Neither the steward and I, nor Mr. Kuran and his friend, could move the professor from the quay into the caique which, though held against it by its boatmen, was one moment level with the top of the quay and then several feet below. The women wrung their hands. "Oh, poor John. What is to be done?" they whimpered.

Mr. Kuran told me that there was only one solution, and I agreed that we must loose no time and accept it. He hailed a large, powerfully built boatman and Mrs. Gurney and Mrs. Villiers-Stuart cried out with outraged alarm as the professor was hoisted upon this man's back, from where, instead of clutching it, he tried fearfully to dislodge himself.

"Oh, no, *no*!" cried the women. "Yes, *yes*, trust the man!" advised Mr. Kuran. "He is a good man. I know him well. He often does this."

The boatman staggered to the edge of the quay with his terrified, struggling burden. Cries of indignation and encouragement mingled. Children ran about laughing. The man bent his knees and, judging exactly the right moment when the caique had risen level with the quay, jumped into it, dropping the professor on some sacks lying in the bottom.

It was done. We others followed as best we could, assisted by Mr. Kuran and his friend, and called brief good-byes as the caique pulled away, too concerned about the old man lying on the sacks to think of being polite and properly thank Mr. Kuran for all he had done for us.

The German freighter had turned into the wind and the *SS Proleterka* loomed ahead, with all the lights on the decks making a fine show and the colored lanterns glowing cheerfully above the dance floor in the saloon. The flags at the bow and on the masts fluttered in the breeze and the gangway was lowered to receive us.

It proved to be more difficult to transport the professor from the caique to the gangway than it had been to get him off the quay. It was a nightmare fraught with danger, and when it was finally accomplished we gladly gave all the money we had with us to the boatmen who had achieved the feat. Then we pushed, pulled and coaxed the limp professor up the gangway, lifting his feet step by step, the nurse continually whispering endearments and encouragement to him. When he reached the deck, he collapsed into a chair, with his sister and his secretary fussing around him and the nurse ready with water and pills, while I raced to the purser's office to make him turn off the loud, maddening tune of *Happy Days Are Here Again,* to which we had returned aboard.

When the *SS Proleterka* went alongside the quay in Beirut at 5:30 next morning and I was helping the purser prepare the documents, with the lists of passenger names and passport details for the authorities, Professor Garstang's nurse came and calmly told me that her patient was in a coma, his pulse alarmingly weak, heartbeat and blood pressure barely perceptible. I ran to Dr. Young's cabin and made him go to see the professor immediately, which he was most reluctant to do. He returned a few minutes later and said that there was nothing he could do; the nurse was competent and in charge. It was obvious that he did not want to become involved, and he claimed that he had to go on the full-day motorcoach excursion to the Roman temple at Baalbek because some of the lady passengers suffered from stomach upsets and others had sprained ankles that required his professional assistance.

He had greatly disappointed me as a travel companion, and now as the *Accompanying Physician* of the cruise. It is unwise to select a doctor by his good looks and charm.

Mrs. Gurney and her son and Mrs. Villiers-Stuart remained on board, as did the excellent Mary Gough, who helped the nurse in looking after her patient, and who presently came to me and told me that Professor Garstang had died. She said she had closed his eyes and laid him out.

The purser, extremely displeased when I brought him the news, contacted the authorities by radio and soon a doctor from the Department of Health came on board to certify that death had occurred due to natural causes, not by any infectious disease requiring the ship to be placed in quarantine. Two hours later the body was removed to the morgue. Mr. Gurney went to the British Embassy, taking with him the professor's passport, to request assistance with all the formalities. The nurse would accompany the body by air to England; Mr. Gurney and his mother and Mrs. Villiers-Stuart would continue the cruise. The funeral service and burial beside his late wife would be in the professor's village after they returned to England. Emmy Villiers-Stuart would make all the arrangements with her usual efficiency.

By the time the passengers returned from the Baalbek excursion, I had posted a black-bordered notice on the board in the ship's lobby, announcing Professor Garstang's death. There would be no music in the saloon. The insufferable Professor Burn declared that, in his self-styled capacity as senior lecturer, he would deliver a eulogy after dinner, but the other lecturers over-ruled him and were in agreement that it was more suitable for Mrs. Gough to speak, briefly, since she had been for many years a friend of the professor and his wife and had often traveled with them in Turkey.

"This has been a sad day," she said, "but sad is perhaps not the right word. Professor Garstang was so scarcely with us, so plainly soon to be taken from us, that his actual death, on the day after he had revisited his beloved Mersin, was solemn and moving but not a terrible shock or sorrow. I think he enjoyed the few days he had of the cruise; he was interested and amused by the fact that was actually seeing tourists being taken to the Cilicia, where he had traveled so hazardously and painfully half a century before but where, as he often told me, he had always had a glorious time. It was this capacity to enjoy and be interested that gave him, I feel, a glorious time now right up to the end."

"So no ghastly dance music in the saloon tonight," Professor Burn said to me. "At least poor old Garstang's overdue demise has spared us that. And no visits to filthy nightclubs in Beirut, with no *bakshish* for the Cruise Misdirector. But no doubt little Miss Mary gave you something for letting her have her little moment of glory this evening."

"Oh, come away, A. R.," said his wife. "Let's go over the notes for your important lecture on Knossos tomorrow."

When Mr. Gurney returned from the British Embassy, he said that he had to speak privately to me. I led him into the cruise director's office, where he seated himself importantly behind the desk. "You may sit if you wish," he said.

"Now look here, Ebensten," he began. "I take it that you will not be able to re-sell the professor's cabin for the seven remaining days of the cruise, more's the pity, but I will retain its key to make quite sure that you don't give it to anyone else or make any use of it; but of course the family expect and demand that a refund is forthcoming for the three daily meals that the professor will not eat, as well as for the electric power he will not utilize and for the fresh bed linen and towels no longer required for him from now on. And then there is the matter of water. Fresh water aboard is a major item of expense, as you should know, even if you don't, and I have calculated that the professor would have used no less than fourteen pints of fresh water per diem, so that the cost of ninety-eight pints of water is to be refunded. I have incurred considerable expenses here in Beirut—it has all been most tiresome—so let me have the total refund this evening, to enable me to settle my liabilities before we sail at midnight, and I want it in sterling cash, no fancy foreign currency, together with your itemized statement of the refunds."

He did not wait for my response and I was too stunned to have been capable of making any, as the rich Mr. Gurney strode briskly out of my office.

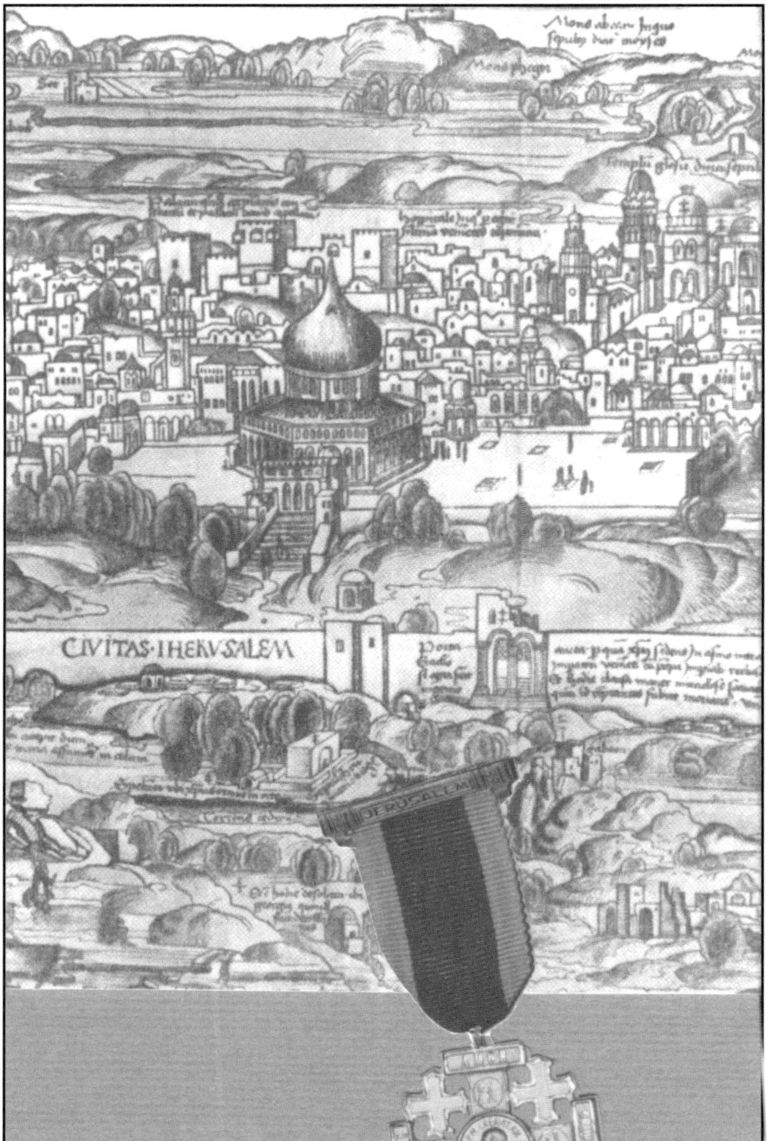
CIVITAS·IHERVSALEM

— 4 —

O Jerusalem

Before I could reach Jerusalem, I was taken into captivity in Iraq, the country that, for many centuries and until the 1920s, was named Mesopotamia—the land between the rivers Tigris and Euphrates, which is, with Egypt and China, one of the cradles of the world's civilizations. King Nebuchadnezzar had kept the Jews there for fifty years, from 587 to 537 B.C., but it was British Airways who took me unwillingly to Baghdad for eleven hours.

It was Saturday, May 1, 1965. The flight from London to Amman in Jordan was delayed more than five hours, so that it was midnight by the time the plane circled Amman's airport, circled once more, and then rose at full speed to a higher altitude, to the consternation of the passengers, who realized that something was not right. The captain announced that the landing lights at Amman were insufficient for a safe night landing and he was taking us on to Baghdad, where hotel accommodations would be provided for the night and from where the Amman-bound passengers would be taken to Amman next morning. All around me my fellow travelers regaled me with the reactions typical of their nationalities. The British were resigned and allowed themselves to show neither anxiety nor concern. The Americans cried out in alarm that they had no visas for Iraq (nor did any of the passengers except those who had planned to go to Baghdad after the short stopover in Amman). Two German businessmen angrily demanded to be set down in Amman and dismissed the problem regarding landing lights as a prevarication of the captain's to save the cost of landing the plane there for the benefit of only a few passengers. The Levantines totally lost control of themselves, stormed up and down the aisle, screamed and shouted abuse, burst into tears and had to be forcibly restrained from physically assaulting the flight attendants.

Half an hour later, when the plane touched down at Baghdad airport, British Airways had everything efficiently arranged. The luggage of the Amman-bound passengers was separated from that of those who had come to Iraq and was not searched, but placed on a trolley to be taken directly to the hotel where the airline had reserved rooms for us. At the Immigration desks, British Airways representatives explained why we had no visas and we were waved through. I was in my room at the Baghdad Hotel by 3:00

A.M., the muddy Tigris rolled by below my window, and at 7:00 A.M., I was awoken with Bed Tea on a tray, in the best British colonial manner, and told that the bus back to the airport would leave at 7:45 A.M. sharp.

By 11:00 A.M. I was in Amman. The driver of the car that had been ordered to meet me at the airport the previous evening had been informed of the plane's delay and was waiting for me. We drove westward across the desert and down to the river Jordan and the Dead Sea.

The Dead Sea! That sea of legends and the Bible was simply a long lake surrounded by barren cliffs, and the fact that the famous Dead Sea scrolls had been found there and that the lake was the lowest place on earth, 1,300 feet below the level of the Mediterranean, did not make it look different than an expanse of water at a less grotesque altitude. As Oscar Wilde said of the Atlantic, I was disappointed in the Dead Sea, but of course I had to swim in it, as I might never come that way again.

My driver stopped at a hotel which was quite deserted, neither staff nor guests being in evidence. I took my swimsuit out of one of my suitcases, maneuvered myself out of my clothes and into it while sitting in the car, and entered the dark, intensely salty water. It was a strange sensation to be in the element in which one is accustomed to have to move one's arms and legs in order to keep afloat, and it was actually unpleasant not to sink but be kept unnaturally bobbing about on the surface. After a few minutes I was glad to return to *terra firma* and a fresh-water shower on the beach was fortunately functioning so that I could vigorously scrape the salt off my body, arms, legs and face and rinse it out of my hair.

And then on and up into the more inviting landscape of Palestine, with gently rolling hills and cultivated fields surrounded by neat stone walls, trees, and flowering shrubs among the village houses. There were no garish advertising billboards along the sides of the road or in the villages we passed, and I was pleasantly impressed to see that all the houses, from the smallest and most humble homes of farmers or shepherds to substantial family residences, were built of the handsome, local honey-colored stone. I later learned that the Palestinian authorities wisely insisted that the country's stone must be used for the exterior walls of all modern constructions so that they would conform with the ancient buildings. New motor roads must be built to follow the contours of the landscape, not insensitively in straight lines, and new villages or extensions of towns are not laid out in a grid pattern but with their streets winding this way and that, and houses not aligned as by a ruler but attractively grouped so that everything reflects a continuance of the unmechanized past.

The road led around the Mount of Olives and then dipped down into the Cedron valley. I asked the driver to stop at the Garden of Gethsemene for my first view of Jerusalem. Before me stretched the huge wall, almost forty feet high and two-and-a-half miles in circumference, enclosing a city set upon a hill and surrounded by deep valleys on three of its sides, that was an unassailable fortress in ancient times. Behind it rose the bulk of the El Aqsa mosque and the golden Dome of the Rock, behind these the slim towers of many churches, and in the distance, silhouetted against the setting sun, the ugly, offensive modern high-rise buildings of the Israelis immediately outside the Holy City's western wall.

We drove on. The road turned right, skirted the city wall, and there was the Damascus Gate, of which I had seen so many pictures, read so many descriptions, that I felt as if I had been there before. I was in Jerusalem.

Some of the porters who were lounging on the pavement outside the gate rushed towards the car as soon as it stopped and unloaded my suitcases. A Western gentleman must not carry his own luggage in an Eastern country. I said good-bye to my driver and the porters asked me where I was staying. I told them I had a reservation at the Dom Polski. They indicated that they approved of my choice, and I followed them through the gate into the Old City. My friend and mentor Stewart Perowne, who had lived in Palestine for thirty years and helped to excavate the town of Jericho, had recommended me to avoid the tourist hotels of Jerusalem—even the lovely old American Colony Hotel, a converted Pasha's mansion north of the city walls—and instead to stay at the Dom Polski, a pilgrims' hospice operated by an order of Polish nuns. Only by being there, within the walls of the Old City, would I be able fully to savor the atmosphere and seep myself in the sanctity of what Pliny, the Roman writer, had said, that it is the most splendid city not only of Judea but of the whole East.

The city's Christian quarter is immediately past the Damascus Gate, and the Dom Polski only a few hundred feet down the main bazaar street, the Souk Khan ez Zeit, past the fruit and vegetable market and vendors of buckets made of old car tires. The nuns looked with alarm and consternation at the suitcases that my porters carried in: pilgrims are not expected to have so much luggage. I was aware that a hospice is not a hotel, but a smile of greeting and a kindly word would have been welcoming at the end of my long journey. Instead, the tight-lipped and grim-faced nuns indicated that I was to place the charge for three days' lodging in advance on the desk and, in exchange for it, they put down the key of my room in order to avoid making even the smallest physical contact with me. How strange it is that good Christians are so bad at communicating with their fellow humans but bestow kindness on animals and plants. I was accustomed to travel in Muslim countries where the stranger is invariably warmly received, regardless of his age, his worldly possessions, and his faith, where the purchase of postage stamps or a can of fruit juice or a slice of melon becomes a joyful event. Not so at the Dom Polski. I went up the stairs, located my humble room, saw a sign in several languages pointing to the bathroom, and made three trips down to the lobby to bring up my suitcases. I realized that I was not a pilgrim but that despised creature, a tourist; but despite the lack of a welcome, I felt privileged to be there, so close to the Via Dolorosa, among the bustle and clatter and shouting in the walled city.

The history of Palestine is indeed a fascinating one. Abraham came to Palestine from Iraq around 1800 B.C. after having wandered for decades with his tribe through Arabia. They did not stay long but moved on to Egypt, where they remained for six hundred years until Moses led them back to the mountains of Palestine, which were occupied by several other tribes—Canaanites, Amonites, Moabites, Jesubites. When David, the second king of the Jews, wanted to settle his nomadic tribe at Urusalim, the city of a god named Selim, he purchased the threshing floor of Araunah, a Jesubite farmer, on which his son, King Solomon, built the first Jewish temple. But we must not be misled by the pompously grandiose title of king that was assumed by the leaders of a small group of people who occupied only a few square miles of Palestine. It was not until the twentieth century that Arabian sheiks extended their tribal territories and aspired to be called kings.

The next centuries were turbulent times for Palestine. Attracted to this rich land flowing with milk and honey—and of bunches of grapes as large as a man (see page 168)—came the Babylonians, led by King Nebuchadnezzar, the Philistines, the Selucids, the Egyptians, the Persians, the Assyrian hordes, Greeks led by Alexander the Great. All of them came, saw and conquered, ruling for some years until each was dispelled by a more powerful invader. In the year 63 B.C., the Romans arrived and created their capital city of Caesaria on the Mediterranean coast. They flattered the Herods of Judea by allowing them to retain the title king, but it was their procurators, of whom the best-known to us is Pontius Pilate, who ruled Palestine in the name of the Caesars. Theirs was a beneficial rule, with the sole exception of the mad Emperor Titus, who destroyed Jerusalem in 70 A.D. In 132 A.D., the Emperor Hadrian rebuilt the city and named it Aelia Capitolina, and that is much as we see it today.

The Roman Empire adopted Christianity as its state religion and, in 326 A.D., the Empress Helena came to Jerusalem to look for places associated with the Bible. Deep under the Roman Temple of Venus, she found a pit with some pieces of wood in it, decreed that it was the tomb and the cross of Jesus, and a great church was built over this spot.

Then the Romans were displaced by other invaders. In 614 A.D., the Persians returned, but in 638 A.D. the Muslims arrived led by Mohammed's formidable warrior, the Caliph Omar ibn al Khattab. Since then, except for three short periods during which the European Crusaders captured Palestine for a total of less than 120 years, Jerusalem has been a Muslim city and all of Palestine a Muslim country, a considerably longer time than it ever was either Jewish or Christian.

Its Muslim rulers came from Arabia, from Mesopotamia, from Egypt, and, from 1517 until 1917, from Turkey, which during World War I sided with Germany, so that Great Britain felt obliged to chase the Turks away and to administer Palestine for thirty years, during which it enjoyed a period of prosperity such as it had not known since Roman times. By the infamous and disastrously ambiguous Balfour Declaration of 1917, Great Britain offered Jews a home in Palestine—not a *land*, far less a *state*. At that time, the Jews there were only eight percent of the population and, like the Christians, during fourteen centuries of Muslim rule had never been persecuted or prevented from worshipping at their holy places. In 1948, the British withdrew, as the Crusaders had done in the twelfth century—they appreciated that Palestine was not their land—but divided it by an Armistice Line between Jews and Arabs, giving the Jews a narrow strip along the Mediterranean coast, most of Galilee, and the large Negev desert which, it was hoped, could be cultivated by using the massive financial aid from America. The Arabs retained all their other land up to the river Jordan. The city of Jerusalem was to be under international control. Alas, the Jews were not satisfied with what had been allocated for them and resorted to violence. They occupied more of the Arabs' land and advanced to the gates of Jerusalem where, from the roofs of their concrete high-rise buildings on the Armistice Line, their machine guns pointed menacingly down into the Old City.

Stewart Perowne had not only recommended me to stay at the Dom Polski but insisted that on my first morning in Jerusalem, even before going to the Church of the Holy Sepulchre, I must walk from the hospice along the Souk Khan ez Zeit to an alley leading off it and enter Zalatino's confectioner's shop and ask there to be shown *el bab*, the gate. The owner or one of his young assistants, Stewart had told me, would immediately take me to the back of the shop, open a door, turn on the electric light and show me the remains of a very large, ancient doorway set in a wall of massive stone blocks, which is the middle entrance of the original triple portal of the Church of the Holy Sepulchre as depicted in the third century mosaic map of Jerusalem at Madeba.

I did as instructed, asked to be shown *el bab,* and the owner did immediately call to one of his young assistants who led me into the back room, opened a door and turned on the light, before walking in front of me down some stone steps into a cellar. Along its sides were large containers filled with different kinds of flour, cases of eggs, and boxes and glass jars of dates, figs, nuts and raisins and honey and other ingredients for making breads and pastries—and there, at the back wall, exactly as Stewart had described it, was the original doorway of the church, still intact with its hinge holes and bolt sockets, through which the Crusaders had entered the church when they captured Jerusalem in the twelfth century. A brief look sufficed to see what remained of it and meanwhile the young confectioner's assistant had lifted his white robe with his right hand and stood smiling at me, fondling his genitals with his floury left hand. Although Stewart had married Freya Stark, the distinguished author and traveler, all his friends were bachelors and he must have told so many of them to go to Zalatino's and ask for *el bab* that the owner and his staff understood quite well what they really wanted to see and do in that sweet-smelling cellar! The boy showed himself surprised and disappointed that I did no more than give his shoulder a fatherly pat, tip him for having turned on the light, and walked back up the steps into the shop where I bought enough pastries to last me for a week.

Then I went to the Church of the Holy Sepulchre and entered it by the small side door where the Arab custodian was stationed, less to guard the church than to try and maintain order among the quarreling priests of many sects that lay claim to the holy places in it. I had read dozens of travelers' tales about the horrors of this most holy of churches, from Kinglake and Curzon, who visited it in the 1830s, to Robert Byron and Richard Halliburton in the 1930s, but none had prepared me for the ghastly reality. It was inconceivably awful in its darkness, its miserable restorations, degraded by the garish, gaudy tinsel ikons, the plaster figurines of saints, the tasteless and undusted paper flowers. Priests glared with hostility at others of a different sect and at the visitors, handling tall candles like threatening weapons. At Easter, I had been informed, these brawling fanatics become hysterical and so violent that battles are fought before the altars and people have been beaten to death. Fortunately, I was not there to witness such scenes, but I saw enough to turn my stomach with revulsion, due only in part to the acrid stench of hot wax, rancid oil and human sweat that filled the air and the discarded orange peels, olive pits, broken water and juice bottles and camera film packages over which I had to walk from one hideous altar to the next, all ornamented in the most execrable taste. There are dozens of altars, shrines and chapels within this church, and over the years, opposing Christian sects have acquired the privilege of serving them—and of collecting donations from visitors for their upkeep. Thus, the Greek Orthodox, the Roman Catholics, the Armenians, the Egyptian Copts and the Syrians all do their utmost to direct visitors to the holy place that belongs to them and do not hesitate to push and pull them in the right direction, to the angry objections of priests who want the bewildered pilgrims to come to their concession and hand out tips, buy candles, trashy beads, crucifixes and souvenirs. Many beggars also operate in the church, until detected and driven out by the priests. The Abyssinians have lost the right to operate within the church and are now relegated to the roof, but they are very sly and mingle with the visitors; one grabbed hold of my jacket and hissed that I must follow him up to the roof to see the most holy thing in the church, his Chapel of St. Helena. I brushed him aside.

The subterranean Tomb, the most revered part of the church where pilgrims fall to their knees and pray, resembles a pawnbroker's shop, with gold and silver chains and pendants and bracelets and watches hanging in a glass case and festooned over a wax figure of the Virgin. The site of the crucifixion is, incongruously, immediately above this.

I found the Church of the Holy Sepulchre offensive enough to make me wish to embrace Islam or become a pagan. It occurred to me that if the priest-merchants in the Hebrew temple two thousand years ago had conducted themselves as did the priests in this befouled church today, it is no wonder that Jesus made himself so unpopular by chasing them out of it. I longed to do the same here and sweep out all those squabbling, abusive, competitive men of God with their vile tourist trash, leaving only the calm, courteous Arab custodian. I could not remain a moment longer in this place of superstitious mummery and falsehood, and rushed away from it to the Damascus Gate, and to the Garden Tomb.

In the year 1883, the British General Gordon visited Jerusalem and, with the Bible in his hand and using it as his guide, much as Schliemann had used Homer's tales to find Troy, wanted to elucidate the true sites of the crucifixion and entombment of Jesus. He knew that they could not have been below the Church of the Holy Sepulchre, in the middle of the walled city. Although archaeological research has shown that during Roman times the walls did not extend on all sides as far as they do now, and that Golgotha—*the place of the skull* in both Aramaic and Hebrew—and Calvary, from the Greek *kranion*, the skull—could have been just outside the western wall as it then was, he did not believe it. The Romans erected crosses for execution on the main roads leading out of their cities, where travelers could be warned by seeing the punishment that had been inflicted on criminals and dangerous political agitators. But even if Jesus' cross had been where the church now stood, it would not have been anywhere near the gate on the western wall, from where the road leads to the port of Jaffa, nor near the more important gate on the north wall, from where the road led to the Roman capital of Caesaria on the coast and to Damascus. The cross had to have been erected elsewhere, where passersby could see and ponder over it.

General Gordon was a friend of Mr. and Mrs. Horatio Spafford, a couple from Chicago who had founded the American Colony, a nonsectarian religious community, in Jerusalem. One day when he was sitting on the roof of their house built against the inside of the city's north wall, he saw a rocky hill a few hundred feet away on the right side of the road leading out of the Damascus Gate, and had an inspiration; it seemed to him that this rock resembled a skull. He hurried to it, and found that its top was big enough to hold three execution-sized crosses. Here was the true Golgotha or Calvary as recorded in the Bible. He was totally convinced, and so were his friends the Spaffords, and his friends Sir Charles and Lady Watson, but he begged them to keep the knowledge to themselves. "We believe it to be true," he told them. "Let that be sufficient." He did not want the true place of Jesus' death to become a hideous attraction such as the Church of the Holy Sepulchre with its priests' unseemly conduct and sideshows. Two years later, General Gordon was killed defending Khartoum in the Sudan; and many years after his death, he was vindicated in his belief by the discovery near this Golgotha of an authentic tomb of the first century. Even if it is not the tomb in which the body of Jesus was placed after the crucifixion, it is exactly the location which a rich Jew like Joseph of Arimethea would have chosen for his tomb.

The place is historically in accordance with what we know and, moreover, it looks right. Despite General Gordon's request that it be kept a secret in order to protect it from desecration, British protestants began to hear about it and came to worship there among flowering bushes and trees, undisturbed by disputatious priests and sellers of tourist baubles, but none was there when I went to it. I was alone in a garden, a holy site as it should be—peaceful, tranquil, a perfect place for quiet contemplation, "a green hill far away, without a city wall, where the dear Lord was crucified, who died to save us all."

It is by wandering around the Old City of Jerusalem that the pilgrim (and the mere tourist) is spiritually and visually rewarded. The first walk recommended to Christian visitors is along the route that Jesus took from the place of his trial to that of his crucifixion. Jews naturally first head for the remnants of the outer wall of King David's temple, knows as the Wailing Wall, and Muslims for the Haram esh Sherif with the El Aqsa mosque and the Dome of the Rock. It is widely assumed that the trial of Jesus before the Roman procurator Pontius Pilate took place in the Pretorium fortress near the northeast corner of the city wall, which King Herod rebuilt and named Antonia in honor of his Roman friend Mark Anthony; but Pontius Pilate also sat in judgement in the Citadel, near the Jaffa

Gate on the west wall, and the trial may have been there. It is irrelevant to argue about the route Jesus took; what matters is that he did walk through the city, along streets where I now walked, streets that have never felt the touch of a wheel, in a city that has not altered in two thousand years, where he heard the same tapping of cobblers' mallets and passed vendors with the same wares as displayed now and saw around him people wearing robes as worn today. He walked, and it may well have been along the narrow street that is now named Via Dolorosa, but the fourteen stations of the cross, which are marked on it by modern signs and numbers and which good Christians follow, are of course a pious fabrication. No one knows and never did know where Jesus fell the first time, and the second time, and the third time, where he was greeted by his sorrowful mother, where Simon the Cyrene helped him to carry the cross, where Veronica wiped the perspiration from his face with her handkerchief. All along the street, priests point out these Stations of the Cross to the visitors, and I watched as devout pilgrims went down on their knees and touched the stones and the signs and the numbers and even kissed them, and paid the priests for having been permitted to do so. On Fridays, the Franciscans with their followers go in procession along the Via Dolorosa bearing small replicas of the cross that do not need, as did Jesus, the assistance of one or two men to carry them.

Throughout the Old City, a locality is assigned to every minute event connected with Jesus, as mentioned in the Bible. Everything is identified, often disputed but venerated, sometimes treated with contempt. Here is the house of the rich man, there that of Lazarus (both are clearly of Arab construction). There is the house of the Jew who would not let Jesus rest and told him to move on, for which act of rudeness he was punished by having to wander about the globe ever since. In this house, Mary, the mother of St. Mark, was baptized and St. Peter found refuge after his escape from prison. Here, in what is now a cistern under the Imperial Hotel, is Bathsheba's pool where Uriah's wife was bathing when King David saw her. Here is a stone bearing a footprint of Jesus—"Yes, you may kiss it if you wish." Even Alexander William Kinglake, who visited Jerusalem in 1835 and who had been brought up on the Bible and was a believer, admitted that "with respect, for instance, to the certainty of the spot where the cock crew, I am far from being convinced."

But by no means is everything within the city associated with the Bible; the Romans left reminders of their stay. The pedestal of a modern street lamp is a column bearing a votive inscription in honor of the legate Marcus Junius Maximus of the Tenth Legion, and some of the city's oldest pottery waterpipes show the imprints of the detachments of the Roman legions who installed them more than two thousand years ago.

The time had now come for me to visit the Temple Mount, Mount Moriah, "the chosen mount." It was on this level and smooth limestone rock that Abraham was prepared to sacrifice his son Isaac. It is the Haram esh Sherif, "the noble enclosure," a flat rectangular space measuring 900 feet by 1,650 feet and constituting one fifth of the city's total area, the thirty-five acres that are sacred to the world's three great monotheist religions and where all the city's authentic history is recorded. Here the first temple of the Hebrews, that of King Solomon, was destroyed by the invading Babylonians in 587 B.C. The second and more splendid temple was built when the Jews returned from their captivity fifty years later and it remained intact until 70 A.D., when the Romans destroyed it and the Emperor Hadrian built a Temple to Jupiter in its place. The site was neglected until 638 A.D., when the Muslims captured the city and identified the rock in the center of the Temple Mount as the place from which, according to the Koran, Mohammed ascended to heaven, and the Caliph Omar erected a simple wooden mosque over it, which was later replaced by the fabulous marble and gold Dome of the Rock. The enclosure has echoed to the psalms of David, the words of Jesus, and the precepts of Mohammed. It proclaims the spiritual brotherhood of man.

I walked along the Souk el Qattani to the Iron Gate in the enclosure's western wall and stepped up into a vast, airy, paved space which came to me almost as a shock, and certainly with a wonderful sensation of relief, after the congestion and confusion and noise of the city—an astounding contrast of peaceful serenity and order, a place of calm refuge for contemplation. And how glorious it was, on this great open level platform, to be able to look up and see the sky, which was obscured within the city due to the narrowness of the streets and lanes, many of which were covered with awnings to keep off the scorching sun, and could only be seen by climbing up to the flat roofs.

Here the great Hebrew temple had stood. Excavations had confirmed the detailed descriptions of it by the Roman writer Josephus who inspected it before its destruction. Here I walked slowly, respectfully, up to the center of the enclosure, to the Dome of the Rock, also named (incorrectly) the mosque of Omar. Together with the El Aqsa mosque built against the south wall, it is for Muslims their holiest place after the Kaaba in Mecca and the Tomb of Mohammed in Medina. It is a large, regular octagon, a shape so pleasing to the eye that I wondered why it is so rarely used for buildings of importance. From within it, raised on columns, is a circular drum topped by the gently swelling, shimmering golden dome that rises to 108 feet above the stone platform, plus another twelve feet to the glittering crescent on the pinnacle. Standing at the center of the Haram esh Sherif, it dominates it as it dominates the skyline of Jerusalem when seen from the Mount of Olives. No one who has seen it has failed to be astonished and thrilled by its beauty. Writers have lavished endless superlatives on it—"the most glorious building ever erected by man"—"the most celebrated of mosques"—"one of the wonders of the world"—"wonderful grace and symmetry"—"enchants visitors of all religions"—"unique." The Greek poet Nikos Kazantzakis rather quaintly likened it to "a gigantic multi-colored male peacock."

The lower half of it is covered with marble slabs, the upper half with blue and golden glazed tiles with geometric patterns. Verses from the Koran, in elegant white Arabic script on a background of dark blue, run on a frieze along the upper edge. Four arcades of slim, graceful columns gently direct the visitor to ascend eight steps to the doors at the cardinal points and to enter the shrine. The interior is circular, the walls are covered with tiles bearing geometric and floral designs. The colonnade that supports the dome and surrounds the sacred rock consists of twelve columns with different bases and capitals, having been taken here from Byzantine non-secular buildings. The plain, unadorned limestone rock, the summit of Mount Moriah, is protected by a circular iron grille. The dome is a vast inverted bowl of glittering golden mosaics. From the arched windows set high in the dome, light filters into this harmonious assemblage of veined marble, lovely tiles, mosaics, and dark carved wood screens and doors. It is indeed an exquisite space and I wandered around in it and absorbed its proportions, its quiet, its unrivalled serenity, and marveled at the superb craftsmanship of its columns and ceilings and doors and stained-glass windows.

Having entered the shrine by the western door, I now left it by the door facing east, where, very close to it, stands a miniature prototype of it, inexplicably called the Dome of the Chain, in which the arriving Muslims housed the Haram's treasury. Then I walked towards the second mosque in the enclosure, that of El Aqsa, and passed the El Kas fountain—"the cup"—shaded by cypress trees, and politely averted my eyes from the men who were performing their ritual ablutions before going to pray in the mosques.

The El Aqsa mosque—the name means "place furthest away" from Mecca, to which, according to the Koran, Mohammed was taken on his miraculous one-night journey—is built against the enclosure wall on the southern section of the Haram esh Sherif, thirteen feet lower than the platform around the Dome of the Rock, on the site of the palace of the Herodian kings of Judea. It is a very large mosque and was designed for communal worship, while the Dome of the Rock is a shrine for individual veneration. Having been built on artificial foundations, unlike the Dome of the Rock which stands on solid rock, it was vulnerable to earthquakes and was twice destroyed during the eighth century and rebuilt as we see it today. In the eleventh century, it was man, not nature, that assailed it: the Crusaders gave it vulgar domestic uses, but since 1217 A.D., it has again been a mosque. Cypress trees stand before its entrance porch, which has seven painted arches, corresponding with the seven aisles divided by columns within it. The interior is all white and austere; the columns, as those in the Dome of the Rock, were moved here from early Christian buildings. The prayer niche—*mihrab*—on the south wall, facing Mecca, is flanked by columns decorated with mosaics. The pulpit—*minbar*—is of ebony inlaid with ivory and mother-of-pearl, very fine. Near the main prayer niche are two others, one dedicated to Moses and one to Jesus, both of whom are sacred to Muslims. It was heartening to see them.

I had heard about a double gate below the floor of the mosque, which is almost the only surviving portion of the Hebrew Temple. When I expressed my interest to see this, a sheik was summoned who, without hesitation or fuss, brought a large key and led me down a long series of steps into a very scantily lit vaulted passage. At the end, there were two openings in the wall, which had been filled by doors more than two thousand years ago.

Another and much larger underground vault is nearby, at the southeast corner of the enclosure wall, well-preserved and supported on a dozen pillars in two rows; it is named Solomon's Stables but was, instead, the stable for the horses of the invading Knights of the Templar during the Crusades in the twelfth century.

Many other, lesser monuments and memorials have been erected on the Temple Mount; all are small and unobtrusive and do not in any way detract from the spaciousness of the great enclosure. The Dome of the Prophet, which almost touches the Dome of the Rock on its northwest side, marks the spot from which Mohammed is said to have ascended to heaven. The Crusaders mistakenly took it to be the place of Jesus' ascension and erected this shrine over it. The Fountain of Sultan Qaitbay, near the western wall, has frivolous decorations that enchanted me, although it has been derided as being "like a pretty tea-cozy." After the plethora of places in the city that are reputed to be associated with Jesus, it was a pleasant change to be shown none on the Temple Mount, but some of the reconstructed sections of the enclosure wall are named for the twentieth-century archaeologists who excavated and exposed them—a dangerous practice in a land where so much is myth, misunderstanding and conjecture. Will tourists in the distant future be shown "St. Robinson's Arch" and "The Prophet Wilson's Arch?"

I returned to the peace and quiet of the Temple Mount four times and it was always a restful retreat from the city streets and crowds. After having strolled among the colonnades, fountains and domed shrines, and the olive, orange and cypress trees, which provided small, refreshing touches of green to the stone enclosure, I then reverently entered the El Aqsa mosque, or the Dome of the Rock, and kneeled on the carpets among the believers. I gazed up to the ceiling and toward the prayer niche and thanked not the cruel god who ordered a father to kill his son in this place nor the wrathful god who threatened to darken the sun and the moon and make the stars fall from heaven, but to my good God, and offered thanks for all the blessings which have been bestowed on me. Here I was not surrounded by distasteful clutter, by frantic kissing of statues and paintings, by intrusive priests with goods for sale. It was not Mammon but God who was worshipped here. Nothing garish or ostentatious distracted me from my devotions, no representations of that naked man writhing in agony on the cross and no sinister maimed, wounded, beheaded saints—and not once did anyone, anywhere in this noble enclosure, approach me with a demand for a gratuity or a contribution. Not once was I offered trumpery souvenirs or false relics. Muslims, unlike Christians in the Holy Land, do not desecrate their sacred places by using them for avaricious and demeaning commercial activities. *El Hamdu Lillah.*

When I had been at the Dom Polski for almost a week, I was determined to find other lodgings. I liked being in the Old City but felt out of place in this pilgrims' hospice with its depressing atmosphere, where I had to communicate with the nuns mostly by signs and a few words of German. It was not unnatural for the devout nuns to move about silently with their eyes always downcast, although I had known nuns elsewhere who occasionally smiled and even laughed; but in the Dom Polski, even the visiting pilgrims looked miserable and unhappy and passed me on the stairs and in the corridor with lowered heads. At breakfast, they sat hunched over their plates as if it was their punishment to have to eat—as indeed it often was, because the meals were singularly tasteless and everything that was provided looked pallid and unappetizing, although just outside the hospice the bazaar vendors offered fine fresh produce, fruit and vegetables, eggs and cheese, meat and poultry and fish attractively displayed. Why did a Christian hospice have to be so dismal, I wondered? Against my will, I felt myself being conditioned to accept a grim way of life that was abhorrent to me. I was afraid to ask the stern nuns for any small favor. There was no glass in my room, so that I could not rinse my teeth after I had eaten, but I dared not request one. When I went to sleep, I began to feel that it was shameful for me to make myself as comfortable as possible in my cot, to turn from one side to the other, and thought that, in keeping with the Christian spirit of chastisement, I must lie flat on my back, legs straight, arms at my sides or crossed on my chest, like an effigy on a Crusader's sarcophagus. No, it was time for me to depart from the Dom Polski. It was either a fortuitous coincidence or fate, when I left the hospice that morning, that a man addressed me. I could tell that he was not a tout or a pimp; he was an Arab gentleman and I guessed his age to be in the mid-fifties. His white kefiyeh headscarf and robe were immaculate and of the finest material, his shoes were well polished, he wore an opulent wristwatch, he spoke English with fluency and was obviously well educated.

He introduced himself as Ahmed Dahoum and gave me his card, with an address in the Old City, as well as a post office box number. This inspired confidence. He asked me where I was going and I told him that I was on my way to the office of Thomas Cook & Son to see if there were any letters for me.

"May I accompany you? We can talk as we walk," he said.

He walked slowly—indeed he glided—in a stately manner, like a prince. He asked if I was happy staying at the Dom Polski and I confided to him that I was beginning to feel oppressed there. What I did like was the roof, where breakfast was served and from which the view over the roofs of the Old City, the Temple Mount, and the Mount of Olives was magnificent.

"How much do you pay there?" Mr. Dahoum wanted to know. I told him it was very reasonable, only one dirham forty girsh per day.

"Including meals?"

"No," I said, meals were extra.

"I can offer you a good, clean room in my own house, a very old, historic house in the Old City, for only one dirham per day. I give no food now in my house, but you can have tea whenever you want. Room is cleaned every day and bed made, fresh sheets and towels twice a week—and from *my* roof you have the same view as at Dom Polski. Shall I show you?"

As he spoke he accompanied his words with the graceful, expressive hand gestures of well-bred Arab men which Westerners can never learn to emulate. I trusted him, and felt safe with him, and it was encouraging to see that he was well known and respected. As we walked along the streets and through the alleys, the shopkeepers, shoeshine boys, vendors, strolling members of the Home Guard in their saffron-yellow kefiyehs, and Christian priests greeted him effusively, some quite deferentially. Children addressed him as "Sheik Dahoum." Once he stopped to talk with a flower seller, picked a wild dog rose, pale pink, deeply inhaled its scent and then presented it to me. I also smelled it and pulled its stem through the buttonhole in the lapel of my tweed jacket. Mr. Dahoum smiled his approval.

He led me across David Street and south into the Haret esh Sharaf quarter to a narrow lane that was no more forbidding than any of hundreds in the Old City, opened a low door and said, "Welcome! This house is your house!" I followed him into a room that was arranged like a doctor's waiting room, with divans along two sides and a low table with Arabic magazines on it. There were ancient swords and other weapons on one wall, and an airline calendar still showing the days of the previous March, with a color photograph of a Swiss chalet almost buried in snow. He gestured me to sit beside him on one of the divans. Two boys, around fourteen years of age, bounded down the stone stairs and he told them to bring us tea and dates.

"You are in the Beit esh Sakka," said Mr. Dahoum, "the house of the water carrier, because in Roman times it was an inn and had on it a sign of Aquarius, the man with the pitcher of water. It was to this house that Jesus sent his disciples to order their Passover feast in the upper room, what Christians call the Last Supper."

"You are not serious, Mr. Dahoum," I replied in amazement.

"Quite serious. General Gordon, who found the real place where Jesus was crucified and put in the tomb, on the road to Damascus outside the city, often came to this house in 1883. He spent many days searching in the cellar and concluded that this is the house where the Last Supper was served; but he told my grandfather never to speak about it to avoid Christians from making it into a place of pilgrimage and worship, with all their sellers of souvenirs and calendars and candles and pictures and ugly statues. 'I believe it to be true,' the General said, 'let that be sufficient,' and my grandfather respected his wish, and so did my father, and so do I. It will never become a Christian shrine; it is an Arab house and my family home."

I was by no means convinced. It was surely no more than a fanciful legend, but I did realize that this humble house in the Old City was far more likely to be the place where the Last Supper had been served than the spurious large cenacle in the fourteenth-century building shown to tourists at Mount Zion outside the city walls. It was, at the time of Jesus, a Hebrew requirement that the Passover feast had to be eaten within the walls of the city.

Mr. Dahoum took me up the stairs to the upper part of his house and I could see by the greater height of the ceilings there that several floors had been added over the years; the lower floor's ceilings were very low, not much over six feet high, with doors through which I could pass only by bowing my head. On each floor, three or four rooms led off a central hallway, and he took me into one of them, which was to be mine. It was about ten feet by eight, with a window looking out to a narrow alley, and contained a bed, a table and two chairs, a dressing table with drawers and a mirror, and wooden pegs on one wall for hanging clothes. Rudimentary but clean washing facilities and an Eastern-style toilet were at the end of the corridor. At the top of the house the stairs opened on to the roof, which had a chest-high wall on all sides, so that I would be able to sunbathe there unobserved.

The primitive washing and toilet facilities did not deter me, and the price for the little room was wonderfully attractive. The door of my room had no lock, but I would always take my passport and money and everything of any value with me when I went out sightseeing or to restaurants, even when I went up to the roof. Mr. Dahoum was a delightful man; I trusted him, and decided to move in the next day.

When I arrived at the house with a porter carrying my suitcases, Mr. Dahoum was sitting in the room just inside the front door with two men who, he told me, were his cousins. He greeted me warmly and called for a boy to bring us glasses of tea, and two other boys took my luggage up to my room. I soon learned that there were at least two other good-looking young boys in the house, all of them running up and down the stairs and along the corridors, in and out of the rooms, never idle, sweeping and washing the tiled floors, cleaning with brushes and mops, making beds, always very friendly and cheerful, often mischievous, occasionally fondling one another in a casual manner.

I never regretted having moved to Mr. Dahoum's house. I enjoyed his company and talking with him, I enjoyed the presence of the polite, ever smiling boys, but I began to wonder who the many visitors were, men ranging in ages, from a few who were young to the majority who were middle-aged and some quite old, all of whom

Mr. Dahoum introduced to me as his cousins—"my cousin from Amman, come to make big business here—my cousin the doctor—my cousin with the Department of Agriculture." I never found out—and do not know to this day—whether the Beit esh Sakka was the home of an elderly roué who liked to have boys around him and offered them to his many visiting "cousins" for entertainment, or if I was staying in a male brothel. There was no sign of impropriety but the boys were always as playful as puppies and occasionally I saw one of them go into or come out of a room with one of the "cousins." I was very content to be there, despite the basic washing facilities and the Eastern-style toilet, to which I never became reconciled. I kept fruit and pastries in my room and whenever I wanted to have a glass of hot mint tea, I had only to ask one of the boys who were running about. They were glad to be tipped for bringing it on a tin tray and never failed to favor me with a big smile. It was all most congenial.

One morning when Mr. Dahoum was not in the house, I went with my flashlight down to the cellar. Some of the boys were curious, but I waved them away. I found that the house was supported on a series of low vaults which were many feet below the present level of the lane and felt certain that I was standing on the Herodian foundations of a house that had assuredly been there in biblical times. If it had been an inn, why should it not have been here that Jesus had eaten his Last Supper? In Jerusalem, anything is possible. I saw no Hebrew or Roman inscriptions on the walls, nor the stone with the sign of

Aquarius that General Gordon was said to have discovered there; perhaps Mr. Dahoum's grandfather had sold it to a museum.

That evening, Mr. Dahoum was very angry with me. "Why did you go into my cellar?" he demanded. I explained that, as an art historian and a writer, it was natural for me to want to investigate the Herodian foundations of the house.

"Please do not go there again. I forbid it. I do not allow anyone to look for old Jewish stones in my cellar. And please do not write about my house. I do not want English and American ladies to come and kiss the walls of the Beit esh Sukka because Jesus ate his supper in it."

I apologized and assured him that I would not write about it. He was not appeased; but a few days later, he had forgiven me my trespass. A peace offering in the form of a vase of red anemones appeared on the table in my room and he invited me to have tea and pastries with him, during which he expressed his disappointment at my showing so little interest in the boys of the house.

"Do you not like my boys?" he asked me. "Not one of them? They are all good, clean boys."

I told him that I liked them all for being so cheerful and keeping my room so clean and tidy.

"Please, Mr. Hanns. We are friends now. You must call me Ahmed. We are men of the world, we understand each other. I assure you, they are good, honest boys."

I told him that I believed it. I never missed any of my belongings, although when I returned to my room I often noticed that things had been taken out of my suitcases and inspected.

"You pretend not to understand me, Mr. Hanns. I tell you, any of my boys will make you very happy!"

"I do understand you, Ahmed, but I do not like boys in the way you mean."

He raised his eyebrows dramatically and turned his eyes to the ceiling in amazement. "*You do not like boys*? But there is nothing shameful in liking boys; it is natural. The Koran promises us eternally youthful boys in paradise. We all like boys and all the Western men who come here like boys, even those that travel with their wives. England's King Richard, with the heart of a lion, and our great Saladin, who fought for possession of this city but respected each other, both liked boys; that General Gordon liked boys."

"Well, I am the exception."

"Now, Mr. Hanns, please do not play a game with me and pretend that you like *girls*!" he said and distorted his face with distaste.

This frank man-to-man discussion encouraged me to be bold and to confide in him; I feel less inhibited to talk about my personal feelings to a stranger (especially to one in a foreign country whom I am unlikely to meet again) than to a friend. "Well, alright then, I'll tell you. I like *men*, men in uniform—policemen and soldiers," I confessed.

Mr. Dahoum digested this information with complete equanimity. "One of my sons is a soldier," he said. "He is a good man, clean and honest. I will tell him to come here tomorrow evening in his uniform and be at your disposal."

I was unable to disguise my astonishment and, seeing this, he added, "It is important, in this life, that we are happy."

Wanting always to be gracious and kind to strangers and guests, Arabs tend to make well-meaning promises but feel no need to do anything further to ensure that they are kept. I put no credence in Mr. Dahoum's words, but when I returned to the house the next evening after dinner, he was having tea with a soldier. "This is my son Mahmoud," he said. Mahmoud was taller than his father, a fine man with superb black eyes, thick eyebrows and a fierce moustache. His smart khaki uniform robe was embellished on the chest and arms with many badges and sewn-on patches and chevrons in bright colors. An impressive bandolier crossed his chest with highly polished cartridges gleaming in its loops. Secured by the right epaulet was a striped lanyard with the whistle by whose piercing sound he could summon more stalwart soldiers to him in an emergency. Strapped to his wide leather belt, where his ancestors would have thrust their jewel-handled daggers, was his powerful handgun. He wore the traditional red-and-white kefiyeh, falling in graceful folds on each side of his head and held in place by the *agal,* the double circle of black wool, the most becoming headgear devised by and for men. I was very happy.

It was a source of continuous fascination and never-ending delight for me to wander aimlessly along the streets and alleys of this walled city which has been described as the most interesting 250 acres on the face of the earth.

Its streets and bazaars were crowded all day and most of the night with people on the move—priests, monks and nuns of every Christian sect, the Armenians and Syrians and the black Abyssinians being the most gorgeously attired, hurrying purposefully or slowly deliberating before making a purchase, politely stepping aside to let others pass and never as aggressive as in their churches; stately princes of the church and dignified imams, a troop of Boy Scouts, four Buddhists in orange robes, the Anglican bishop on his way to his order's pilgrims' hostel near the Citadel, peasants bent under the weight of huge bundles, veiled Muslim ladies attended by their servants, patriarchal Arab sheiks, perambulating vendors of hot tea, cold water and freshly-squeezed fruit juices, ice-cream sellers. Arab gentlemen surreptitiously pulled grubby envelopes out of the pockets of their robes from which, protected by cellophane covers, they extracted small pieces of old leather with Hebrew letters and offered them to gullible tourists, for many hundreds of dollars, as fragments of Dead Sea scrolls from Qumran caves. Shoeshine urchins sat on little wooden stools outside every church and along the city's tourist routes. Beggars lay on the ground, each of whom could have been the Caliph Haroun el Rashid in disguise. Every type of business activity was carried on out of doors—shoemakers, tailors, barbers and dentists were busy in the streets in front of their tiny, unlit cubicles.

I am not a compulsive shopper and in Palestine planned only to buy honey and spices and one small item of piety, but studying the wares so artistically displayed in the shops and on the vendors' barrows provided me with hours of entertainment. In the Souk esh Shamma were thousands of red, blue and ornately gilt candies, baskets filled with incense and dried rose petals, and thorns twisted into the shape of Jesus' crown on the cross. In the Souk el Husr were traditional pipes and flutes as still used today by shepherds, Greek ikons painted on gilt panels, straw hats and flywhisks. In the Souk el Zeit were pyramids of pink and pale blue toilet rolls, jars and bottles of weird cosmetics and medicinal lotions, mountains of herbs and spices, trays with assorted pastries soaked in honey and rose water, and earthenware pots ranging from the size of thimbles to some large enough to conceal one of Ali Baba's thieves. Handcarts were piled high with flowers, fruit, vegetables, books in many languages and mostly in states of total collapse, radios and electrical equipment, bales of textiles of wool, linen and cotton, plain and striped and encrusted with gold and silver threads, toys both traditional and modern. Fortune-tellers and magicians and musicians strolled about. Little girls shyly held out a single flower to tourists, or pocket calendars, or color pictures of saints cut out of magazines, mounted on cardboard and varnished to look precious. Fruit and vegetables were being constantly sprinkled with water to look appealing and tempt the palate. Vendors polished their apricots and tomatoes and aubergines to give them a fine shine, plunged bunches of grapes into buckets of water to refresh them, and rubbed figs and dates between their fingers, one by one, to soften them. Melons and oranges were displayed cut in half to reveal their juicy flesh.

I knew of course that not all Palestinian Arabs are Muslims and was given proof of this when the young vendor from whom I regularly bought the fruit for my room turned up the sleeve of his gray robe to let me see the cross tattooed above his wrist. "I am from Bethlehem," he told me.

Arab men held each other's hand as they walked or sat smoking water pipes. An English woman in a café watched them with fascination and nudged her husband to point it out to him. "Means nothing here," he told her.

I could not resist saying, "It means a lot. It means that they are brothers, or cousins, or *friends*." The couple turned away from me. English travelers abhor being addressed by strangers, particularly concerning delicate subjects.

I discovered unexpected aspects of city life and watched young boys—and some not so young—merrily splashing each other and screaming with joy in a shallow, rectangular pool of water called The Patriarch's Bath. Near the Beit esh Sukka, in one of the confusingly winding lanes, a group of Kara Goz dancers performed their traditional, robustly lewd antics on most evenings, not for tourists—who rarely ventured into this bewildering maze and never after dark—but for the people who lived there. I admired their strange and beautiful musical instruments and asked to be told their names. That shaped like a long-handled banjo was a *basuq,* the lute was an *el'oud,* the zither a *qanun,* the one that resembled a fiddle was a *rababa* and the drum was a *dabaka.* The players persuaded me to try and play the drum, while onlookers applauded my dismal ineptitude.

Stewart Perowne had told me to go and see the Armenian's Cathedral of St. James but my experience at the Church of the Holy Sepulchre had made me wary of entering other churches in the city. However, I always do what my betters tell me, and went there. Tourists rarely explore the Armenian quarter, which is off their usual route at the southwest corner of the city; the gallery of Armenian Art attracts almost no visitors to it. The Armenian convent is vast, a city within a city, and houses the residence of its Patriarch, chapels, schools, hospices, and a library where I was shown a genuine relic—the amber scepter of the last King of Armenia. Christians today are apt to forget—or wish to ignore—that theirs is an Eastern religion, reaching pagan Europe many hundreds of years after it thrived in Palestine, Syria, Egypt and distant Abyssinia. Armenians were converted in the third century and came to Palestine, and the interior of their cathedral is as austere as a mosque, which it resembles in its restraint of decoration and quality of peace. Its walls are tiled, silver lamps are suspended from the ceiling and hang low over the floor, as in mosques, and the floor is carpeted, also as in mosques. The congregation sit on the ground and during services walk about reverently, as Muslims do. Stewart had been right, as he generally was, to advise me to go there. Nothing was false or contrived for cheap effect, nothing was in bad taste; but here, too, albeit to a far lesser degree than in the Church of the Holy Sepulchre, the priests and their pert, ingratiating acolytes repeatedly pestered me with requests for money and attempts to sell me rubbish. In this respect, the Cathedral of St. James did not resemble a mosque.

One morning, Mr. Dahoum was leaving the Beit esh Sakka at the same time as I and he asked where I was going. I told him that I was on my way to see the Wailing Wall. He was surprised. "You have not yet been?" I, too, was surprised that, for some reason quite unknown to me, I had put off going there. "May I accompany you? We can talk as we walk," he said.

The western wall of the Temple Mount is part of the retaining wall that was built by King Herod, and Jews come there to pray and mourn the destruction by the Babylonians and the Romans, respectively, of their first and second temples.

So there we stood, he and I, side by side before this famous wall. How fortunate are the Jews who, instead of having to try and worship in false and hideous places among grasping priests, are able peacefully to pray in the open air facing this authentic and undisputed wall of King Solomon's Temple, mellowed by three thousand years of veneration. This wall is also sacred to the Arabs, being part of the Haram esh Sherif from where Mohammed ascended to heaven. It is far more impressive than I had been led to believe by written accounts and photographs of it, sixty feet high with nine courses of gigantic stone blocks; the topmost rows of stones are smaller than the others, having been added in the nineteenth century by order of a British philanthropist, Sir Moses Montefiore, to prevent the upper edge from crumbling. But no Jews wailed and prayed there that morning, as they should have been. It is their place. Why were they not there?

"My father was a Jew," I told Mr. Dahoum, curious to see what his reaction would be.

"I thought so," he said. "You are most welcome in my house. The Jews are our cousins, we have lived side-by-side here for fourteen centuries and never harmed them. Why are they not here, praying before their wall? We never prevented them from doing so. Abraham and Moses are as sacred to us as to them."

He spoke the truth. Ever since the Muslims, led by the Caliph Omar, captured Jerusalem in 638 A.D., they have been protected. In 1187, Saladin encouraged more of them to settle there; in 1492 those that came from Spain were welcomed and many Jews became Arabic-speaking. In the eighteenth century began the great influx of Jews from Russia, Morocco and Yemen.

"We never sent them away," said Mr. Dahoum, "but now, after fourteen centuries, our good neighbors decided to leave us and throw in their lot with the foreign Israelis from the West, whom we hate because they are taking our land away from us."

"Perhaps the Israelis will go away after ten or twenty or eighty years, as the Crusaders did," I said.

"*Inshallah*!" intoned Mr. Dahoum.

I parted from him there and went to the Hammam esh Shifa, only two hundred feet away. I went once or twice a week but had never told him about it because I did not want him to know that I found the washing facilities in his house unacceptable. He probably knew that I went there, as also to the Hamman el Ein, because they were close to his house and he had spies throughout the Old City who kept him well informed of anything that might interest or concern him.

Both these baths were close to the wall of the Hebrew Temple and many feet below the present level of the streets, and may have been ritual baths used by Jews two thousand years ago before entering the precincts of their temple. Arab men of all ages came here to sit on the slatted wood benches in the steam rooms, sluiced one another with icy water, and relaxed on divans made up with sheets that were none too clean and discussed business matters and disputed about politics. They were extremely decorous and kept their private parts covered at all times with towels and ragged clouts. Tattered towels hung on overhead lines to dry in the hot air. The boy attendants brought tea when requested and scrubbed the floors with hard brushes and then washed away the dirty water. I never felt totally clean after my visit and was always the only foreigner there, but was made to feel welcome.

Since Mr. Dahoum had instantly recognized me outside the Dom Polski as a man who would be happy in his house of Aquarius, and as I was now an inmate of the house in which Jesus had eaten his Last Supper, I thought that it was fitting that I go out of that house after my supper and follow in Jesus' footsteps to the Garden of Gethsemane. I ate pastries and fruit in my room and then walked out of the Old City through Herod's Gate and down the Cedron valley to the base of the Mount of Olives. The Garden of Gethsemane is the only authenticated place in Jerusalem where Jesus walked. The eight olive trees are still there; they were subjected to tests in 1947 by a botanist who stated that they are almost three thousand years old. Alas, the Franciscans have thought it fit to enclose them by a wall with a locked gate and have laid out geometric paved paths and bricked-in enclosures planted with ridiculous flowers that are not even native to Palestine. It is sacrilege indeed. However, there is the garden to which Jesus and his disciples went after their Passover feast—but why did they go there? It was April and a very cold night (the altitude is 2,500 feet above sea level). Jesus was staying in the village of Bethany, just up the Mount of Olives, so why did he and the disciples not go to their snug lodgings for the night? Why, instead, did they wander about in that dark garden? Men's habits have not altered in the East—or anywhere else—in two thousand years, and today, as then, men go out in the evening after a good dinner to parks and gardens outside the city walls in order, in Colonel T. E. Lawrence's words, to slake one another's needs in their own clean bodies. Jesus and his disciples were healthy, active young men; surely there is nothing reprehensible in their having gone to a well-known place of rendezvous that night?

The Gospels, which romanticize and sanitize everything, are especially obscure in relating the events that are said to have occurred in that garden.

Not being able to enter it, I could, however, wander about close to it, among other ancient trees and caves on the slope of the Mount of Olives, where many men had come looking for partners. It was very dark, and the flitting figures, most of them in robes and some in Western clothes, could not be seen clearly, so the men would stand still for a moment, strike a match or light a cigarette lighter in order to enable those who pursued them or showed interest in them to see their face and, if it was considered to be pleasing, to come nearer. It was all exactly as I had observed it in parks and gardens outside cities from Morocco to Tunis to Egypt to Jordan.

When Jesus came here after the Last Supper, his disciples behaved disgracefully to the man who was their leader and had been their host. They left him and dispersed to seek privacy for their activities in the caves and grottos, so that he had to go to them three times and urge them to "pray, lest you enter into temptation"—but it was surely in the quest for sensual adventures that they had gone there that cold night. "The spirit is indeed willing, but the flesh is weak," Jesus told them. Then Judas came into the garden and, not having seen Jesus since he left the supper party early—probably to pay for the food and wine, being the group's treasurer—he gave him a loving kiss of greeting. Men habitually kiss each other in the East and no doubt did so then. Jesus was well known in Palestine to people of every kind, and to the authorities, and it did not require a kiss for him to be recognized. When the soldiers came to arrest Jesus, Judas said to them, "Get him safely away"—not the words of a man who has betrayed his friend. Poor Judas has been much maligned for almost two thousand years.

Only three of Jesus' disciples did not run away. But what of that curious young man, wearing a linen cloth cast around his naked body, who makes his appearance in the Gospel of St. Mark? Why was he there, if not also in search of sexual gratification? He remained by Jesus' side, but when the soldiers grabbed his skimpy garment, he shook himself free, leaving the linen cloth in their hands, and ran off naked into the darkness. Who was this mysterious naked young man?*

When I told my new friend Mahmoud that I would soon leave Jerusalem and that, before I did so, I wanted to see something of the Palestinian countryside and visit Jericho, Hebron and Bethlehem, he said he would ask for a day's leave and get permission to use one of the army jeeps.

---

* The English philosopher and jurist Jeremy Bentham, in his early-nineteenth-century interpretation of the Bible, refers to him as "a stripling clad in loose attire" and assumes that he was a *cinaedus*, a male prostitute.

I explained that I was surfeited with churches and ancient historic places and planned to make only very brief visits to the towns. I wanted to walk in fields, meet local people and drink tea or coffee with them. He understood me. "It will be my pleasure to show you my country, and my friend Hussein will come with us. He is from Hebron and can visit his mother and sister."

I was thrilled by the prospect of making the excursion with him and Hussein, and he named the day on which I was to meet them outside the Damascus Gate at eight o'clock in the morning. "I will bring bottled water and fruit," he said.

Mahmoud had brought his friend Hussein along one evening when we had arranged to meet at the Beit esh Sukka and, on the pretext of being on duty, he had left me alone with him—and that was not the only one of his dashing fellow soldiers to whom he had introduced me. "The entire army corps seems to be finding its way to my house," said Mr. Dahoum benignly. The indifference with which these Arab soldiers treated our meetings greatly appealed to me. There were no false words of endearment, no tedious preliminaries, no sentimental leave-takings. Apart from a brief moment of pleasure, they were as uncomplicated and devoid of emotion as drinking tea together or sharing an orange and, when it had been eaten, throwing away the peel.

One evening, when I returned to the house later than usual after dinner at the American Colony Hotel, Mr. Dahoum was sitting in the downstairs room with a scholarly gentleman, wearing Western clothes, and two soldiers. He did not ask me to join them but indicated that I was to go to my room. "Goodnight, Mr. Hanns," he said. "Professor Habib and Mahmoud's friends are waiting to go up and be with some of my good boys."

The army jeep was at the Damascus Gate at the appointed time with Mahmoud and Hussein in the front seats. I was to sit behind them where I would be more comfortable. Mahmoud had brought bottles of water and a melon, and also a red-and-white army-issue kefiyeh for me—not only decorative but eminently practical to protect the head from the fierce sun and the wind and to provide warmth after sunset, when the air quickly became chilly.

It was exhilarating to be driven around Palestine in this open army jeep, guarded by my two identically uniformed warriors. I was not quite Lawrence of Arabia—it was fifty years too late for traveling by camel—but it was a romantic journey nevertheless. Mahmoud and Hussein conversed almost entirely in Arabic, but I did not feel ignored. They pointed out places to me and stopped the jeep whenever I asked them to do so, usually remaining in it to smoke while I walked across fields and in the shadow of trees. In villages, when I invited them to have tea or coffee with me, Mahmoud always insisted on paying. "You are in my country and guest," he said. I did not want to stop anywhere along the road from Jerusalem to Jericho, and as we descended from 2,500 feet above sea level to 1,300 feet below it (3,800 feet in less than an hour),

Mahmoud and Hussein put on a great show of plugging their ears with their fingers, but I felt no discomfort. In Jericho, the climate was almost tropical and we passed banana plantations. Mahmoud wanted to show me the eighth-century palace of an Arab sheik, but I preferred to be taken to see the excavations that prove that the town dates to the Bronze Age and is said to be the oldest continuously inhabited town on earth, although places in the fertile valleys of Mesopotamia, Egypt and China have similar claims. It was in about 1250 B.C. that the Jews captured Jericho and its walls came tumbling down; Mark Anthony gave the city as a gift to his beloved Queen Cleopatra of Egypt.

On our way up to Hebron—it is at a higher altitude than Jerusalem—we passed orchards of light green almond trees, darker green carob trees, apricot trees with white flowers, and the ubiquitous evergreen olive trees. On narrow strips of cultivated ground, I saw onions, leeks and cucumbers. There were many vineyards here, and it was from this region that Moses' spies are said to have brought him a bunch of grapes as big as a man, to prove to him how fertile the Promised Land was. The bunches I picked were of a more modest size and when I offered the farmer's boy some money for them, he at first smilingly refused to accept it, but when I persisted, reluctantly pressed it into his pocket. I greedily ate one bunch and took the others to Mahmoud and Hussein in the parked jeep.

Hebron possesses a shrine that is sacred to both Jews and Muslims because it is the burial place of Abraham, and thus has within it a synagogue and a mosque, whose close proximity has caused strife and bloodshed. The huge exterior walls are of Herodian masonry and show how the walls of the far larger temple in Jerusalem must have looked.

Hussein left us here to visit his family, and Mahmoud and I drove to a garden owned by Russian Orthodox priests, where we asked for permission to rest in the shade of the oak tree under which Abraham is said to have rested, and where we ate Mahmoud's melon. He smoked and dozed until we returned to town, where Hussein was to meet us at the shrine. He arrived there with his heavily veiled mother and two young women and a lively little boy, either his nephew or his son (it was never made clear to me), who wanted to be given a ride in the jeep, but Mahmoud would not permit it and the mother had to console him. She and the young women were laden with melons and bunches of grapes, which they stowed them behind the jeep's back seat. None of them spoke or understood English, but by means of gestures and smiles and some helpful translation by Mahmoud and Hussein, I was able to communicate with them and I much enjoyed meeting this rural Palestinian family. They stood in a row and waved when we drove off.

We saw many plantations of trees by the road between Hebron and Bethlehem. Those of eucalyptus trees did not interest me, not being indigenous to Palestine. They thrive in many countries to which they have been introduced from their native Australia, and those in Palestine were all grown from seeds sent a hundred years ago to

Mr. Horatio Spafford, the founder of the American Colony, by a friend in Tasmania. But I did want to walk in the shade of the oaks and the Judas trees that were in full bloom, and, when we were almost in Bethlehem, had to ask for the jeep to stop for me once more, so that I could walk across a grassy meadow where biblical shepherds watched their flocks at night. If Mahmoud and Hussein thought that all my wanderings were stupid, they gave no indication of it and were indulgent and patiently waited for me.

Hebron is a town of Arab Muslims. Bethlehem, only eighteen miles from it, has been an Arab Christian town for almost two thousand years—so much so that, early in the nineteenth century, when Palestine was ruled by Egypt, the Khedive Ibrahim gave orders that every Muslim was to be banished. Many have returned since then and built mosques, but they have remained a minority. Christian Arabs who emigrated to North and South America and prospered there have added to the great wealth of the inhabitants, which accounts for the town's splendid mansions, convents, hospitals and Orthodox and Latin churches. Far more church towers than minarets rise above the roofs of the town.

Mahmoud parked the jeep in Manger Square, outside the Church of the Nativity, which was filled with the motorcoaches of tour groups.

The church is a rugged fortress erected over the alleged birthplace of Jesus, but is also the place where King David was anointed and Benjamin was born, and where Baldwin the Crusader, the first Christian king of Jerusalem, was crowned in 1101 A.D. I feared that the horrid scenes I had witnessed in the Church of the Holy Sepulchre in Jerusalem would be repeated here, and as soon as I entered the church through its low door, I saw that my foreboding had been justified. I had to stand in a long line of American, European and Japanese tourists and shuffle slowly towards the gate of the subterranean grotto, while Greek Orthodox, Roman Catholic and Armenian priests and monks solicited us for money contributions and pressed ugly candles, shell-encrusted boxes and other trash on us. Having nothing else to do as they waited in line, many of the tourists made purchases and there was a great deal of haggling over prices and making correct change. In one corner of the grotto is a stone manger and a silver star is set into the floor to mark the site of the nativity. Devout pilgrims pushed aside the hovering Greek, Roman and Armenian guardians, who wanted to be tipped for pointing out relics, and knelt to kiss both the manger and the star.

Having seen the main attraction of the church, I did not stand in the lines that formed to be shown the lesser sideshows—the Orthodox altar of the circumcision and the rivaling Armenians altars of the three kings and the Virgin. Those who delight in casting doubts on the Gospels point out that a grotto is not a stable, and mangers are not made of stone, and argue that all the churches in the Holy Land stand on sites that have no historical authenticity but were chosen arbitrarily to provide their quarreling guardians with a steady income derived from pious pilgrims in return for granting them the promise of spiritual comfort and absolution of their sins. They do not differ from gambling casinos, which hold out the promise of acquiring quick wealth: in both establishments the cash keeps rolling in, making the operators rich.

Alexander Kinglake preferred Bethlehem to all other places in Palestine because it was as much a Christian town in 1835 as it is now, and he was enchanted to see unveiled "maidens" and "romping girls" who gladdened his soul by holding his hand and laughing, something no Muslim women did, or do now. I admire Kinglake but do not agree with him in this respect. In Eastern countries, I prefer to see the heavily veiled bundles of mystery that are demure, cherished women, with only their dark, heavily kohled eyes exposed and their slender, delicately shaped and elegantly tattooed hands.

I invited Mahmoud and Hussein to eat with me at one of the outdoor cafés on Manger Square and insisted that I would be their host and pay. I ordered omelets, a stack of the local flat bread, freshly-squeezed orange juice, pastries and coffee, and admired the good table manners of these simple fellows. Two American women, members of a tour group that was assembling to board their motorcoach, saw me sitting there between two armed soldiers and asked, "Hey, are these guys protecting you, or have they arrested you, or what's going on?"

"I am their officer," I told them.

My two companions were greatly amused.

We drove back to Jerusalem and I said fond farewells to Mahmoud and Hussein outside the Damascus Gate and, for the last time, grasped their strong brown hands. When I returned my kefiyeh to Mahmoud he was quite upset: it was a gift. (I still have it, and treasure it, almost forty years later.) I told them that I looked forward to being with them next time I came to Jerusalem.

"*Inshallah*!" said Mahmoud.

"*Inshallah*!" said Hussein.

It had been a blissful day. I will never forget; it was made especially unforgettable for me by the easy fraternization between two Muslims and a man from the distant West, a relationship of mutual friendship and esteem that had first developed in this land between the soldiers of Saladin and those of King Richard the Lion-Heart in the twelfth century. I often wonder if my two gallant warriors realized how much pleasure their congenial company gave me on that drive in their open army jeep. I walked through the gate into the Old City and had to stop for a moment because I was blinded by my tears of happiness.

Before I left Jerusalem, I wanted to take home from it something meaningful in remembrance of my visit—not only the wild dog rose that Ahmed Dahoum had given me and which I had pressed between the pages of Hoade's *Guide to the Holy Land*, nor the red-and-white bobble-fringed army kefiyeh that Mahmoud had given me—but a token of my pilgrimage, for it was in the spirit of a pilgrim that I had traveled to Jerusalem. The holy places of Islam had moved me far more than those of Christendom, but I was nevertheless a pilgrim. Jerusalem had also granted me secular enjoyments that I had never expected to find there; but I remained at heart a pilgrim; and so I dressed very neatly and went to the Franciscan's St. Saviour Convent to apply to the Most Reverend Father Custos for the decoration called the Cross of Honor for pilgrims to Jerusalem, which Pope Leo XIII instituted in the year 1900.

How well I was received there, such a welcome contrast to my experience with the nuns at the Dom Polski! No questions were asked about my religious belief, but neither was the granting of the decoration and its accompanying testimonial a matter-of-fact transaction like obtaining a passport. I chatted with the father in the most friendly manner, he asked me what I had seen and accomplished in the Holy City, how long I had been there, and I did not have to prevaricate to supply satisfactory replies. He enquired where I was staying and I told him that I had first been at the Dom Polski but moved to an Arab house, also in the Old City. "I am staying with Muslim friends," I said. "I hope that does not shock you?"

"Not in the least. St. Francis, the founder of our Order, was always well received when he lodged with Muslims. As you know, in Cairo the Sultan el Khamil wanted to please him and sent a young lady to his room." I was able quite truthfully to assure him that my Muslim hosts in Jerusalem had sent no young lady to *my* room. He shook my hand, and the Cross of Honor was mine, presented to me with his blessing in its neat, square, blue leather box bearing in gilt letters the words SIGNUM SACRI ITINERIS HIEROSOLYMITANI under the Jerusalem cross, which consists of a cross with four crosslets, regarded from very early times as reminders of the five wounds of Jesus, and were worn as the insignia on the tunics of the Crusaders. The silver cross is attached to a red, white and gold ribbon and I proudly wear it on formal occasions. *Crux dum orbis volvitur stat.*

On my last evening in Jerusalem, I dined with Mrs. George Antonius at her house above the Wadi el Joz. I had left two letters of introduction there soon after my arrival in the city, one from Mrs. Coggin, wife of the Archbishop of York, the other from my friend Stewart Perowne. It was a very great honor and a privilege to be invited there.

Mrs. Antonius was a very old lady, the widow of a distinguished Palestinian Christian who had played a leading role in the Arab National Movement and whose book, *The Arab Awakening*, had become a classic. She fled from Jerusalem to Beirut in 1948 when the Israelis bombed her house at Sheik Jarrah, a beautiful residential suburb north of the Old City with the mansions of rich Palestinians and foreign diplomats, but had returned and now lived in a more modest house. Hers was the spirit, and the conscience, of Palestine.

"And how is dear Stewart?" she asked me when I arrived. I told her that he was very well. "Still scribbling away about all the Herods and Caesars and Saints, I suppose. Such a mistake for a confirmed bachelor of fifty to have married. Dear Freya was sadly disappointed."

For almost sixty years, Mrs. Antonius had been the foremost hostess of Arab Jerusalem and had entertained princes, bishops, generals, scholars, writers and politicians, and she was still as warm-hearted but candid as Stewart had described her to me. This evening, her guests included a Saudi prince, half a dozen of whose picturesquely garbed and armed retainers squatted in the garden, where food was brought to them; the esteemed writer, Mr. Walid Khalili; one of the curators of the Palestine Museum; and two Arab social workers and educators—Miss Hind Hussein, a Muslim, and Miss Elizabeth Nasir, a Christian. The youngest was Mr. Ghalib Budeiri, a teacher at the Dar el Awlad, an orphanage for boys that Mrs. Antonius had founded. He and I were the lightweights of this serious-minded gathering of intellectuals. The evening was memorable for me, not only the meal, but the unforgettable conversation to which I listened with spellbound attention, and have good cause to remember in view of future events.

When all the guests were assembled—and how late most of them arrived! In Europe it would have been considered shockingly rude—we sat on cushions or padded stools around a very large, low table on which more than forty different dishes of *mezzes* were arranged in rows. Mrs. Antonius and the two other ladies kindly explained them all to me. Most of the guests took small portions of all or almost all, but I always select three or four that particularly appeal to me, eat many of these, and ignore the others. My favorites this evening were *tabbouleh,* a salad of chopped parsley, tiny green and white onions, radishes, tomato and mint, with nutty-flavored ground wheat; a *hummus* of mashed chick peas, crushed sesame seeds, garlic and lemon juice; aubergine slices grilled over an open fire; and flat, round cakes of minced lamb with *burghal,* ground wheat, pine kernels and many spices that not even Miss Hussein and Miss Nasir could identify. We ate the *mezzes* by tearing bite-sized pieces from the disks of flat bread and used them to scoop up morsel after delectable morsel. There were carafes of white and red Lebanese wines and, for the Muslim guests, Palestinian pottery jugs filled with iced fruit juices and sweet rose water.

The conversation was dominated by Mrs. Antonius' and her guests' views on the Israeli-Palestinian conflict caused by the infamous Balfour Declaration of 1917, of which all those present around the table knew the exact and ambiguous words in which Great Britain, although it did not own Palestine, viewed "with favor the establishment in Palestine of a national home for the Jewish people...it being clearly understood that nothing shall be done which may prejudice the civil and religious rights of existing non-Jewish communities in Palestine." It mentioned *a* home, not *the* home, not a *land,* not a *state.* It envisaged a small place of refuge with a chief world Rabbi, something like the Christians' Vatican City in Italy. The declaration was meant as a friendly gesture, like that made by Mark Anthony, the ruler of the Roman Empire, when he gave Queen Cleopatra the town of Jericho, not all of Palestine. And in that same year of 1917, when Great Britain openly promised the Arabs that, as soon as they had been rid of their Turkish overlords, all the lands from the Mediterranean Sea to the Persian Gulf would be theirs, Britain and France secretly agreed to divide these lands between them under the terms of their Sykes-Picot Agreement. "Dear George always called it a shocking document," said Mrs. Antonius.

The servants in their white robes, most of whom had been trained at Mrs. Antonius' orphanage, now removed the *mezze* dishes, swept the table clean, and ceremoniously carried in a large metal tray with a mountain of rice, which they placed in the middle of the table and then set the main dishes of this feast around it. We had the choice of the ubiquitous *shish kebab*—chunks of leg of lamb alternating on the skewers with oblong, highly spiced meat balls and thin medallions of lamb slit and stuffed with parsley, pine kernels and hot green peppers. There were also, in a shallow bowl, grilled lamb chops on a bed of vine leaves. A salad of cos lettuce leaves was most refreshing.

The Saudi prince greatly feared the steady, relentless encroachment by the Israelis. "Those ugly, high, concrete and steel towers of theirs stand before the wall of our third holiest city and soon they will surely advance and push us further away. We hear their cry 'Next year in Jerusalem' and next year, or the next, they will be here, not only in Jerusalem but all the way to the river Jordan—and, who knows, with their aggressive spirit and all the wealth of

America, this alien race from the West will invade our Eastern lands all the way to the Tigris and the Euphrates and claim Iraq for their homeland because Abraham came from there."

"You are too pessimistic, dear Saïd," said Mrs. Antonius, trying to calm him.

"Not at all. Israel is a colony of America, and how the Americans would love to own our oil!"

"You must take the long view, dear Saïd," Mrs. Antonius advised him." The Jews' attempt to create a Western state on our Eastern soil will fail as surely as did the Kingdom of Jerusalem which the Europeans tried to impose on us and which lasted less than one hundred and twenty years. Remember that, and be comforted. We must be patient. Israel is very powerful now, but the predominance of the Arabs and our immense natural resources must, in time, reverse the balance."

"And not only that," added another guest, "but Israel will self-destruct. There are already indications of that—all those angry dissentions in their parliament, and the despicable treatment by which they antagonize the pathetic dark-skinned Jews from Morocco and Yemen that they brought there and use like slaves. They breed faster than Western Jews do, and will take charge; and they do not dislike us."

"The Western Jews who come to Israel are no longer the Jews who lived here peacefully among us for thousands of years," said Mr. Khalili. "They come with imperialist, materialistic ideas, with revolutionary ideas of conquest. They want to dominate, to drive us away by terrorizing us—and it is all done with the blessing and the money of America."

"But why do the Americans hate us so much; the British always liked us," said one of the lady guests.

"So did the Americans in the past. Mr. Rockefeller liked us so much that he gave us twenty million dollars for our museum," said the museum curator, "but now they have given the Israelis enough atom bombs to enable them to destroy every Arab country."

"It is a Jewish conspiracy," said the prince. "When President Woodrow Wilson appointed his King-Crane Commission in 1919 to study and advise on the future of Palestine, its members concluded that the project of making Palestine a Jewish commonwealth should be given up; but subsequent presidents gave in to the pressure of their rich and influential Jews, and President Harry Truman frankly said, 'I do not have hundreds of thousands of Arabs among my constituents' and allowed the Jews to dislodge and exterminate the people who had been in possession of their land here for fourteen centuries. So now, Israel is a festering sore on our Arab land and the Americans will have to accept the dire consequences of having ignored the recommendations of their own King-Crane Commission."

"The foreign Western Jews will never find peace in Palestine," said Mrs. Antonius. "They should return to America, which they have made their new homeland."

"But even there, they are not accepted in the best hotels and golf clubs," gloated the prince.

The servants removed the debris of the main dishes, again swept the table clean, and now spread a plain white cloth on it and carried in almost as many pastries and desserts as the starting *mezzes*. Instead of trying them all, I made a selection, helped by Mrs. Antonius, to whom I confessed that I doted on sweets, and who explained that the shape of many of the pastries indicated their ingredients. I always find the incredibly rich *baklava* irresistible, and this was diamond-shaped, filled with ground walnuts and finely chopped pistachios steeped in honey, flavored with cinnamon and lemon juice. I also tried—for the first time—pastries shaped like birds' nest, filled with candied grapes, dates and nuts; and there were lemon and orange sorbets to help clear the palate and bowls of fresh, cooling quinces, pomegranates, and figs. Coffee was served in small cups without handles, with as much sugar as anyone could possibly desire.

I made my only contribution to the conversation when, on being asked for my opinion about Israel, I told them that my father, who was as vehemently opposed to the creation of a Jewish state in Palestine as were many Jews of his generation, had always said that he would consider only one position in a State of Israel—ambassador in London.

"A wise man, your father," said the prince and moved across the room to engage me in a private conversation. Being the scion of a noble family—the prophet Mohammed was his ancestor—and blessed with one of the greatest fortunes in the world, he made it a rule to demonstrate his humility by giving courteous attention to the most insignificant and poorest person in any gathering he attended. He asked me about my travels and showed particular interest in the descriptions of my stay with Sheik Barakat's family in the Sinai Peninsula. I told him how much I regretted that, not being a Muslim, I could not visit Mecca, not even the rock tombs at Medain Salih, of which I often read in Charles M. Doughty's wonderful *Arabia Deserta*.

"But when the Israelis have conquered my country you will be able to visit Mecca," he said. "Yes, *you* will be permitted to go, it is I and my people who will be forbidden to worship at the Kaaba. The Jews will claim it as *their* sacred place because, as you know, it was built by Abraham."

"Surely that will never happen, Your Highness," I said.

"Yes, it will, it will. The ambition of the Israelis has no limits. They claim Iraq as their homeland because Abraham came from there, and they claim Egypt as another homeland because Moses was born there. All of Arabia will be theirs, with the approval of the oil-greedy Americans, and their capital will be Kaybar, where their ancient fortress, the Kasr el Yahuda, still dominates the Hejaz."

"Your Highness is too pessimistic, as Mrs. Antonius said earlier this evening."

"Not at all. Katy is out of touch with reality and, fortunately, she will not see it happen in her lifetime; but you, my friend, and I will see it. Remember then what I told you tonight."

When I said good-bye to Mrs. Antonius and thanked her for her gracious hospitality, she said, "Please give my best wishes to dear Stewart, but I hope you are not darning his socks."

I was dumbfounded. "No," I said. "What do you mean?"

"Dear Stewart has been looking all his life for someone to darn his socks. I believe that's why he married dear Freya, but she had other ideas. He was more fortunate when he stayed here thirty years ago with dear old Lady Watson who had been looking all *her* life for confirmed bachelors to darn their socks; she began by darning General Gordon's."

Mr. Ghalib Budeiri left Mrs. Antonius' house when I did and walked with me towards the Old City.

"How long will you remain in Jerusalem?" he asked.

I told him that I was leaving the next day. "This was my Last Supper," I said.

"And a very fine one, too. And now, after your last supper in Jerusalem, will you go on to the Garden of Gethsemene, as bachelors like us have done for two thousand years? If so, I will be happy to accompany you."

I thanked him but explained that I was leaving very early next morning and had to pack. He asked at which hotel I was staying and I told him that I was in the Old City.

"Oh, I see—the Casa Nova, or the Dom Polski?"

"No," I said. "I was at the Dom Polski, but I moved to a private house."

"A private—oh! So *you* are the writer who likes soldiers and is staying with my naughty old friend, Sheik Dahoum! No wonder you do not have to seek adventures when you have all the delights of the East provided right in your house!"

Mr. Ahmed Dahoum was up unusually early to bid me good-bye and I was touched by this last act of courtesy. He had been a good host, and I hoped that I had been an equally good guest. There was much for which I sincerely thanked him, and I hope that he will remember me as kindly as I remember him.

He had ordered or coaxed two of his boys to carry my luggage to the Damascus Gate and out of the Old City, up the Nablus Road past the Garden Tomb and to the Mandelbaum Gate. *Mandelbaum* means "almond tree" in German, but there never was an almond tree there, nor a gate. It was merely a prosaic, open space on the property of a rich Mr. Mandelbaum, which the Israelis and the Arabs had agreed as being a convenient location for the only point of entry and exit between their portions of the cruelly divided Palestine. Barriers marked the limits of each state, with the Arab flag on one side and that of Israel on the other, separated by a hundred feet of no-man's-land. Many months before, in London, I had applied for and been granted permission by the authorities of both countries to use this crossing point on a specified date and hour. Few travelers use it and vehicles were not permitted to do so, except consular cars with the flags of their countries prominently displayed, and the white jeeps of the United Nations observers, who were responsible for ensuring that the uneasy truce between Israelis and Arabs was respected.

The two boys placed my suitcases on the ground by the guarded fence on the Arab side, where we had to say farewell, and hurried away from this place of shame as though from hell. My passport was checked against the list of persons who had been given permission to cross over that day and at that hour, and then I had to walk with my luggage the hundred feet toward the checkpoint on the Israeli side. I had to make two trips to do so and was alone each time, in limbo between enemy lines.

The Israelis were rude, as I had been warned that they would be, treated me as if I was a dangerous invader and grimly searched my luggage with excessive zeal; but they had my name on their list.

My first impression was of shock. After having become accustomed to Arab Palestinians, who always dressed modestly, it was unpleasant to see so many men and women wearing grossly abbreviated clothes that revealed their bare legs and arms, so offensively inappropriate in the Holy Land. But this was Israel, a country of monstrous highways, industrial developments and military installations imposed upon a land that had been, for centuries and until twenty years before, a beautiful agricultural region whose inhabitants had cherished their traditions and done nothing to mar or destroy them, and from which they had been driven into exile. No authority here ordered that new buildings had to conform to the ancient style and be built of the lovely local stone, as in Arab Palestine; no one here prevented the streets and the countryside from being defaced with vile advertising signs. It was a country preparing to wage a war of aggression on its neighbors. The land that had flowed with milk and honey was now awash with guns and money.

All was hustle and bustle and ugliness and confusion. And over it all, I saw the flags with the menacing six-pointed emblem, as sinister as the swastika. Instead of having chosen the seven-branched candlestick or an olive branch for their flag, it was indicative of the Israelis' combative nature that they had adopted the ferociously spiked metal head of a medieval mace. As I was driven down to Lod airport, I longed for the flags with the gentle, benign crescent and the small, kindly star that had fluttered over Jerusalem.

18 East 31st Street

19 Vandam Street

— 5 —

At Home in New York

On Wednesday, October 26, 1966, when the Cunard Line's *Queen Elizabeth* brought me from Europe to New York, I received my first, and, as it happily turned out, my only disappointment with the United States. It was the sight of that puny Statue of Liberty, dwarfed by the tall towers of Manhattan that the ship was approaching. The clumsy pedestal on which she stood was higher than the metal figure; and she was *green*, not a good color for any statue. The torch which she held up in her right hand would have been suitable to serve the lighthouse for which the statue had originally been intended, to stand by the sandy shore of Egypt and guide ships towards the entrance of the Suez Canal when it opened in 1869; but by 1874, the French government had decided to send it as a gift to the United States. It had been packed into 214 crates and sent across the Atlantic in a French warship, reassembled on its pedestal and unveiled there by President Grover Cleveland in October of 1886. So there she stands, an archaic incendiary Greek goddess incongruously misplaced on the shore of a continent she never knew, and, to add insult to injury, so distressingly viridian. No wonder that Franz Kafka, writing about his arrival in New York and having instinctively realized that the torch was a mistake, described the grim lady holding a *sword* in her upraised hand.*

My friend Brian Kenny, having traveled by air via Canada, joined me a few weeks later and we rented a large living loft above the synagogue at 18 East 31st Street off Fifth Avenue, a nondescript area of Manhattan lacking the charm of Greenwich Village and the splendor of the Upper East Side. But for us, its main attraction was a big terrace at the back, which, although surrounded by tall, ugly brick walls, we made attractive by planting fast-growing ailanthus trees—the Chinese Tree of Life—and with many pot plants, and where we sunbathed and ate most of our meals. Being protected from New York's icy winds by the tall surrounding buildings, the terrace was warmed by the sun even on many winter days.

Until the crates with our treasured belongings crossed the Atlantic by freighter—my Biedermeier desk and my Meissen onion pattern china and the precious Tzaroukis

* I became less censorious of Madam Liberty ten years later, after I had seen the far larger and grotesquely ugly titanium statue of the Soviet matron with a sword in her uplifted right hand standing guard on the hill beside the river Dnieper near Kiev in the Ukraine.

etching, Brian's Malaysian bamboo tables and his family silver tableware with the mother-of-pearl handles—we began life in New York with just our clothes and a mattress on the floor.

I had been recruited by Mr. Lars-Eric Lindblad and his wife Sonja, whom I had met in London, to join their very highly regarded travel organization as vice president for tour development. When they first made the offer, I felt myself too settled in my ways to move from the Europe I knew so well to that strange, vast, albeit thrilling, America. Although I had enormously relished my first look at New York in the winter of 1959/60, and Brian and I much enjoyed two subsequent visits, I was now forty-two and no longer a single, roving male but one half of a devoted couple; but when Lars-Eric and Sonja repeated the offer six months later and created a position for Brian to take charge of the company's mail room, we carefully considered the advantages and financial benefits of relocating in the New World and unhesitatingly accepted.

We were stupefied to observe the wasteful habits of New Yorkers in what Mayor John Lindsay decreed to be known as "Fun City." I was brought up in Europe to be thrifty, and when I told one of the girls at my office that I was going to the Salvation Army's second-hand furniture store next Saturday morning to look for bargains, she was scornful. "You're not going to *buy* furniture for your apartment!" she cried. "Listen: wait till Tuesday night and go to the East 60s and 70s and get all your stuff there."

Always inclined to accept advice, I asked her whether there were auctions on Tuesday nights at the Upper East Side, but she grew quite impatient with my ignorance. "Gee, no—but Wednesday morning the garbage gets collected there, and everyone is always redecorating and puts out the old furniture and things the night before."

And so Brian and I went, and we looked, and true enough there were many fine pieces to be taken off the sidewalks; but since neither of us cared for the fussy, ornate Louis-style, and felt too new in New York to surround ourselves with Early American pieces, and considered neither Spanish Colonial nor 1930s Functional our kind of background setting, we moved our nocturnal operations downtown to less fashionable Houston and Canal streets where simpler, sturdier furniture and discarded household goods were always stacked after dark. It was also a shorter distance from there to carry the tables and chairs, rockers, the coffee table, picture frames and bookcases to our loft. We were not desperately poor, but it did seem to us to be a great shame to let so many useful things go to waste. When furnishing for free, unless one waits long in the hope of finding exactly what one hopes for, it is of course impossible to plan too much. We never wanted to have a bright green carpet nearly filling the dining space of the loft, but when we saw a 12 foot by 16 foot rubber-backed, thick-pile carpet with no faults discarded in Carmine Street, the temptation was too great, even though we had to match further acquisitions to that difficult, vivid grass color and pass by many fine cast-off cushions and upholstered armchairs that would clash with it.

When the loft was equipped in this way with all essentials, including glassware, cutlery in faultless taste and two stunning matching table lamps, we began to devote our nightly expeditions to scavenge among the trash piled as if for inspection beside the brimming garbage cans. What a wealth of happy hunting it offered us! We thought it was going too far to salvage toothpaste and shaving cream tubes still more than half full, and we did not bother with electrical appliances that would require hours of work to function well—but the clothes and the reading material became the joy of our new life in this rich New World.

The streets of New York might not be paved with the proverbial gold, but its garbage made the city resemble the legendary Land of Cockayne, where little roast pigs ran about with knife and fork stuck in them and whole mountains were of marzipan. We could not conceive who threw out such fabulous, barely worn clothes in perfect condition; but there were few nights when we did not succeed in finding a pair of lightweight trousers without a single tear which fitted one of us to perfection, or a couple of shirts with not a single button missing, a sweater with a modish stripe, a windbreaker, or some towels, all free, gloriously free, apart from the negligible expense of the Chinese laundry. We stocked our closets with great deliberation and took only garments of the latest style which suited us, knowing well that nothing makes a man appear more a gentleman than his clothes. Indeed, I preferred to continue to wear my old English suits and jackets rather than select anything common or vulgar from the streets, and consequently became the envy of my office colleagues and admired by my secretary. "What an elegant new shirt, Mr. Ebensten," she said, and probably wondered how I could do it on my salary.

The books and the glossy magazines that were stacked on or beside garbage cans more than anything impressed us with the wasteful affluence of our new home. The latest and most fashionable publications appeared on our coffee table—*Venture, Holiday, Sports Illustrated, The New Yorker*—all pristine, unthumbed. In poor old Europe, such magazines were bought only by the very rich and guarded carefully as status symbols, and if they were loaned to an ill friend, he was politely reminded to return them, and ultimately they were mailed to a relative in Australia.

A press agency heard about our scavenger hunts and sent a reporter to interview and photograph us, and articles titled *A Thrifty Pair* appeared in magazines and newspapers all over the United States, from New Orleans to Portland in both Maine and Oregon, to the consternation of some of our friends, with pictures showing us searching trash cans for clothes, carrying home discarded chairs and tables and lamps, and other rejects of America's affluent society displayed on our bed.

When we were settled in with all our old and new belongings, our landlord paid us a courtesy visit, and I anxiously awaited to see his reaction to my large Arabic hanging that covered one wall from floor to ceiling, with an inscription of a phrase from the Koran on it. "I hope you are not shocked to find this above your synagogue, Rabbi Scheinberg," I said.

"*Shocked?* Why should I be shocked? We are *cousins*!" Wonderful, tolerant New York.

When our scavenging forays around Manhattan were over, Brian and I continued to explore the city on our bicycles, and on Sundays we often set off early in the morning to pedal around Central Park, ending with breakfast at the cafeteria in the small zoo. Our friends and the staff at Lindblad Travel, Inc. heard about these outings and began to join us, and in the spring of 1967 we decided, for the fun of it, to call ourselves the Cyclones and I bought two dozen electric-blue nylon windbreakers with white elastic cuffs and waistbands and our club name in white on the back

THE CYCLONES

We met every Sunday, weather permitting, at 10:30 A.M. at the corner of Broadway and West 61st Street, where those who owned no bikes could hire them from the friendly Bicycle Club of America. Half a dozen girls from the office were among our regulars. We were interviewed in the park by the press, and photographed, and this time Brian's and my friends did not have to be mortified to see pictures of us in the New York papers.

On Sunday, October 22, 1967, we arranged to vary our outing by cycling to Lower Manhattan and Prospect Park in Brooklyn. As we crossed the Brooklyn Bridge, a car crashed into some of us and did not stop, but was apprehended for speeding as it left the bridge at the Brooklyn exit. Stella Howland, one of the girls at my office, and I were most seriously injured. I was concussed and bleeding profusely and was rushed by ambulance to the nearby Beeckman-Downtown Hospital, where my distraught Brian waited while I was taken directly into the operating room. A nurse came to give him a progress report. "I'm afraid we'll have to amputate one of your friend's legs, it's too badly mangled," she told him, which made him sick; but a few minutes later, the surgeon came out to him, one of those wonderfully capable, brusque and often brash New York women who are totally confident of their professional ability. "Your friend's going to be O.K. I'm saving his leg. He'll be outa here in a month." (In fact I was there for exactly six weeks, receiving excellent treatment, care and therapy.)

The company-appointed lawyer who was suing the drunk driver of the car that had run down Stella and me was most upset with the superb Dr. Elinor Suitor when she stated that my leg and my other injuries would heal completely, and that I would be able to walk and ride my bicycle and ski again as well as before. "Can't you at least say that his leg will be just *one inch* shorter than the other?" he pleaded with her. "If you do, I can squeeze out at least ten thousand dollars more in damages for your patient." Those wonderfully shrewd, avaricious New York lawyers!

My secretary came to my hospital room every morning with my mail and I dealt with all my work and communicated all day by telephone with the office, which occasionally put calls through to me from clients, airlines and foreign suppliers. When I was released from the hospital, I immediately returned to the office, having learned how to go down into the subway on my crutches and, at the end of the working day, back up out of it. I soon hobbled all over Manhattan and one evening during a light snowfall, when I stood on the sidewalk, held up between my crutches and hoping that an unengaged taxi would pass by to take me to a dinner to which Brian had not been invited, a police car screeched ominously to a stop. "Where you headin', bud?" and, when I told them, "Hop in, we'll give you a free ride." Those wonderfully helpful, cheerful New York cops!

When I had recovered as completely as Dr. Suitor had promised, the Cyclones resumed their Central Park circumnavigations, but on Sunday, August 16, 1971, we made a special Insomniac's Bicycle Tour in collaboration with Miss Celeste Holm's Friends of Central Park, for which we met in front of the Plaza Hotel at the crazy hour of 2:30 A.M. We were led by Mr. Harold Breen, a landscape architect, on a five-mile ride down Fifth Avenue to the Battery, with many sidetrips for visiting historic buildings and parks specially opened for our night-time expedition.

I thought that by then I knew the island of Manhattan, but I had never appreciated its beauty, its magnificence, until we slowly cycled through it that night, with streets bare of traffic and almost no noise, nothing to detract us from studying the architectural merits of the great edifices and the lovely small parks, squares and gardens. I learned a lot from Mr. Breen and discovered a city of which I had never been truly aware.

I had crossed the Grand Army Plaza, outside the Plaza Hotel, hundreds of times without having given a glance at the figure of Abundance on the top of the Pulitzer Fountain, nor did I know that the man on the iron horse was General Sherman. I knew tiny Paley Park, that haven of tranquillity for office workers, off Fifth Avenue on East 53rd Street, and had often sat on its metal chairs during my lunch hour and watched the cascading waterfall that muted the city's noise. It was closed on Sundays, but by special arrangement was open to welcome the insomniac bikers and never looked more beautiful. I had walked innumerable times from Fifth Avenue to the outdoor restaurant in Rockefeller Plaza that was turned into a skating rink in the winter, but did not know that this narrow, paved lane with its series of ornamental pools and flower beds is named the Channel Gardens because it separates the British and French buildings of the complex; nor, at the next stop of the tour, did I know that the marble lions that guard the entrance of the Beaux-Arts building of the New York Library are named Patience and Fortitude. Mr. Breen led us on a detour here to adjoining Bryant Park, where the homeless men and women who lay under the trees and bushes were roused from sleep by the invasion of the cyclists.

The exterior of the pretty little English Gothic-style Church of the Transfiguration on East 29th Street was familiar to Brian and me, as we lived only two blocks from it. We knew the story of how it earned its nickname in 1870 when the pastor of the grand Marble Collegiate Church on Fifth Avenue refused to hold a funeral service for an actor and suggested that the disreputable thespian's relatives should try "the little church around the corner"; but we had never entered it and gladly did so now, when it was opened for the group by prior arrangement. It is noteworthy for its stained glass windows dedicated to famous American actors—Edwin Booth is represented as Hamlet.

We next stopped at Madison Square, where the first baseball games were played in 1845, and where one arm of the Statue of Liberty, complete with the torch, was displayed in 1884 before the statue was erected in the harbor, and from where that extraordinary 21-story Flatiron Building appeared like a vast, slender ocean liner about to steam up Broadway. At Union Square, which was until 1836 the northern limit of the city and where General Washington rides on horseback and, on another statue, Lafayette strides on foot, we turned east to visit Gramercy Park, which was laid out in 1831 in imitation of a London square and, as in London, only the owners of the fine houses surrounding it had access to it. It is still a private park but was opened for us, and here we saw another statue of the actor Edwin Booth as Hamlet.

As we approached the financial district, Mr. Breen scorned City Hall but allowed us ample time for one of the highlights of the tour—the Woolworth Building, whose owners had not only opened it for us but provided coffee for the multitude. Built in 1913 by Cass Gilbert, it was the tallest edifice in the world until the Chrysler Building on East 42nd Street was completed in 1930. Its Gothic turrets and spires soaring to the sky give it the appearance of a cathedral, which in fact it is—a cathedral of commerce. Its Gothic theme is continued in the heavily ornamented lobby, three stories high, with a vaulted ceiling covered with mosaics in the Byzantine style and frescoes of religious scenes. Mr. Breen pointed out the decorator's little jokes under the crossbeams of the ceiling—busts of F. W. Woolworth counting his nickels and dimes, and Cass Gilbert holding a model of the building.

Nearby, we saw the 110-story twin towers of the World Trade Center, which had recently been completed, the Karnak Temple of the New World; but after having viewed the stateliness and refined grace of the Woolworth Building, only few of the insomniacs expressed admiration for those vulgar, grossly large square monsters. It was a relief to go on to Trinity Church, at the top of Wall Street, whose bronze doors, inspired by those of the Baptistry in Florence, were thrown open especially for us. It was founded by a charter granted by Britain's King William the Third in 1679 but burned twice, so that the present church dates to 1830. Its bell tower, 280 feet high, dominated Lower Manhattan until the late nineteenth century, when high-rise office, bank and insurance company headquarters replaced the earlier low houses. Classical music sounded as we toured the interior of the church and in its museum we were shown exhibits of New York from colonial days to the present time. In the adjoining churchyard many famous New Yorkers are buried; we saw tombstones bearing the names of Dutch and British seventeenth-century settlers and of signers of the American Declaration of Independence.

Wall Street, where the Dutch governor of what was then New Amsterdam built a wall of wood planks in 1653 to protect the little town from the marauding Indians and which had become the chief financial center of the entire globe, looked eerily deserted as we pedaled along it to our last stop of the tour, the aluminum and glass tower of the Chase Manhattan Bank. It contains 65 stories, five of them being below the street level and the lowest reputed to be the world's largest vault, longer than a football field, filled with fifty billion dollars in securities and five million dollars in cash for current needs. Twenty thousand people work in it and many of them come down to relax on its private esplanade, which has a Japanese water garden and fountains and Jean Dubuffet's sculpture group, *Four Trees*.

And now the night was almost over, as we rode on to the southern tip of the island of Manhattan into Battery Park, facing that glorious harbor, with the Statue of Liberty dimly discernable on her island, as the eastern sky became pearly pink and the sun rose. Vendors of many kinds of food and drink had been alerted about the dawn arrival of a hundred hungry bicyclists and did a thriving business, but the Cyclones had brought along their own cucumber, salmon and paté sandwiches wrapped in tin-foil, traditional donuts, paper napkins and cups, and champagne to toast the completion of an unforgettably wonderful night during which I had been made acutely aware that this city, often foolishly derided as possessing no past and being crudely new, has a history of more than three hundred years. Wonderful *old* New York!

When Brian and I wearily pedaled up First Avenue with Pamela Doyle, the most congenial of my office colleagues, I saw a friend of mine slouching along in filthy and ripped blue jeans, work boots and a battered cowboy hat, looking horribly disheveled after one of his frequent nights of dissipation and squalor in the cellar of the notorious Mineshaft club. "Good God, there's Ron Keith!" cried Pamela, who knew him as a respectable staff member at the office of the British Travel Association. "Whatever can he be doing, looking like that, at this hour of the morning?"

We waved to Ron but did not stop. I told Pamela that he had a second job, working nights at a construction site.

One morning at the office, I was summoned to the reception desk to try and calm one of the company's most valued and influential clients, who had stormed in and indignantly thrown her air ticket on the counter, crying, "This ticket is wrong, *wrong*, and I refuse to use it! It has the name Isabel Bunker on it, but I am *Mrs. Arthur Hugh Bunker* and that is how it must appear on all my travel documents."

I took her into one of the conference rooms, offered her a glass of sherry, and apologized profusely. "Our ticketing manager erroneously used the name as it is in your passport, which he saw when he applied for your Indian tourist visa," I explained. "I will have this ticket re-written correctly immediately and in future, all your tickets will show your married name—but of course I know that you are Isabel Leighton, the author. One of my favorite books is *The Aspirin Age*, which I often re-read and which has helped me so much to understand America."

And thus we became friends, and she was very good to me when I started my own travel company. She not only entrusted me with making the arrangements for all her travels, but recommended me to many of her friends, so that I sent Gettys on my tour to view polar bears at Churchill, Manitoba, and Roosevelts to snorkel at the San Blas Islands off Panama. This was all highly gratifying. but her own travel requirements were never very profitable for me because, like many exceedingly rich people, she bought only her air tickets (unless she was a guest in a friend's private plane) and her accommodations, ground transportation, meals and sightseeing abroad were provided by those with whom she stayed—a princess in Rome, a French countess who rented a villa in Marrakech every winter, the United States ambassador and his wife in Santiago, Chile, where her late husband had owned all that country's copper mines. Her brother-in-law was Ambassador Ellsworth Bunker in South Vietnam and when she returned after visiting him, she told me, "Until you've been pampered by the U.S. Marines, you don't know how good life can be."

She also told me that it made a bad impression when I answered the office telephone myself and that I must always have my secretary do so—but Sir Richard Musgrave, for whose rental villas in Greece I was the North American representative, said: "What I like about you is that, when I get on the blower, you answer it instead of some ignorant underling." So I often disregarded Mrs. Bunker's well-meant advice in this respect. She treated Brian Kenny as my spouse and invited us together to dinners at her apartment in River House, New York's most exclusive and prestigious residential building on the East River where, despite the fact that it was carefully guarded, she was robbed one evening in its private courtyard when she returned from a farewell dinner for Rudolf Bing at the Metropolitan Opera. Two armed men forced her to give them her jewelry while a third held his gun against the doorman's head. "I was glad for my belief that it's not safe to wear expensive jewelry in New York," she told the press. "I wore effective jewelry, but not intensively valuable jewelry."

She successfully vetoed Gloria Vanderbilt's application to purchase an apartment in her building. "She wears blue jeans and no brassiere and goes about with a black man and all kinds of disreputable jazz musicians. We cannot have a woman like that in River House," she said. Wonderfully exclusive, elitist Upper East Side New York!

When a new edition of *The Aspirin Age* was published, she presented me with a copy inscribed:

> *For Hanns Ebensten,*
> *who has made the worldways I've trod*
> *a delight to travel on.*
> Isabel Leighton Bunker

When I bought my little house in Key West in 1977, she told me with pride that her son-in-law's house there had a brass plate of the Old Island Restoration Association on it's gate and was included in the house tours; and I did not disconcert her by telling her that so had mine.

One of two other Lindblad Travel, Inc., clients who became a friend was a journalist whose weekly column, in which he reported on the current theatre, cinema and television, fashion and fine food and drink, was syndicated in forty newspapers. He was celebrated chiefly in homosexual circles and doted upon by rich ladies who were not, but strove desperately to be, considered as fashionable leaders of society. He was totally without education and when he made his personal appearance before predominantly female audiences, he delighted his listeners with his carefully rehearsed, folksy way of talking, stressing his humble origins, saying *mah* garden and *mah* readers, and addressing women and men, young and old, his social superiors and servants indiscriminately as *honey* and *dahling*. He is no longer as well known as he then was, no longer discusses flower arranging with First Ladies and bishops, but still flourishes, so that I call him Harley Quinn, a name that suits him well because he was flippant, extremely vain, loquacious, witty and theatrical. He was proud of his athlete's physique but spoiled the image of masculinity by wearing trousers that were too tight, and many rings and bracelets, which indicated to all except the most unsophisticated that this self-made man from the backwoods of Arkansas was one of the girls.

And there was Brendan Tuck, a member of the South African delegation to the United Nations who, when he was having his apartment repainted, moved for a week into the Plaza Hotel and invited Brian and me there to have brunch with him in his suite facing Central Park. He asked us for our preference of dishes but we left the selection to him and he called room service for orange juice, coffee, sweet rolls and *oeufs florentine* for five persons, so that we assumed that two other guests were expected; but presently only one entered from the bedroom—but he was quite the largest man I had ever seen, a swarthy bodybuilder professionally known as Turk. His superb muscular development was shown off by skin-tight blue jeans and a black T-shirt. He was the modern equivalent of the immensely strong and virile and totally brainless circus giant whom Parisian ladies of high society had hired for the night in the 1920s. After having been introduced to us, and when he returned to the bedroom to reconstruct his hair, our host said: "So now you see why I had to order two portions for him. What with that and everything else, this week is costing me the best part of my fortune, but I decided to treat myself to the biggest suite in the Plaza and New York's biggest hustler. Not that he actually *does* much in bed, but I love to loose myself in those gigantic arms of his."

Turk ate his two portions but rarely spoke. He was going to spend the afternoon being photographed with Diana Vreeland, the arbiter of style, and seeing that the sun had come out and it was a fine, warm September day, he concluded that his massive legs would be shown off to better advantage in white jeans, so went to change.

When Brian and I left, the elevator attendant asked: "Where you gents in the suite with that big body-builder?"

We told him yes, we had had brunch with him.

"Oh, man, I'd do *anything* to give that guy head," he said. Those wonderfully uninhibited, outspoken New York men!

At 7:00 P.M. on Friday, April 2, 1971, the doors of the Grand Ballroom of the Hotel Waldorf-Astoria were closed. Women had been strictly excluded, and 1,283 men took their assigned seats at a hundred and forty tables and posed to face the red light in the corner near the ceiling for the group photograph. A large sailor piped aboard the guests of honor, who filed on to the speakers' platform, and, to the accompaniment of lusty sea shanties, reindeer savouries were served. By the time after-dinner coffee was handed around, there was much going to and fro amongst the tables. Old gentlemen who had not seen each other for years hugged, punched one another playfully in the ribs, linked arms and broke into song. Naughty stories were exchanged. Youngsters were introduced into the magic circle and presently a spotlight was turned on to two tables up in the balcony where twenty deserving Boy Scouts rose and bowed to the applause in their honor.

A homosexual convention? A meeting of the Gay Liberation Front? No, Mr. Lars-Eric Lindblad had taken a table for twelve at the 67th annual black tie dinner of the select Explorers Club, an all-male association of which he was a member, and I was one of his guests.

Young, middle-aged and old bachelors, married or widowed, these diners were happiest on occasions when women were absent, and although they could not live in a completely male world, they relished every moment in which they could freely exchange raunchy tales of masculine adventure and exploration. Mellowed by rich food and plenty of alcohol, there were tears in many an eye of these mighty men of commerce and finance as the handsome, humble Neil Armstrong—"the last man to leave Tranquility Base"—received an award and expressed thanks on his buddies' behalf and returned to the toast master the little club flag that he had taken with him to the moon.

The toast master was Mr. Lowell Thomas, whose 1919 lectures about Colonel T. E. Lawrence had launched the "Lawrence of Arabia" myth. He wore a dinner jacket with a great amount of gold embroidery and introduced the evening's first speaker, telling us enthusiastically about Captain Irving Johnson's youth, how he had sent for a Charles Atlas course in body-building, grown as strong as a giant and, when at sea, had only to take off his shirt and reveal his mighty muscles to quell a mutiny. Captain Johnson rose and the audience clamored for the ancient hero to strip. He did not do so, but told us with manly gusto about the glorious days of sail and all its dangers endured and triumphs shared, and how one of his German sailor buddies nearly died on the mast beside him but was miraculously saved.

The second attraction of the evening was then introduced. Captain Alan Villiers was also a traditional bluff seadog and, with Churchillian snarls and commands, he extolled the tough life under sail upon the cruel sea and dwelt with relish on the hardships and privations of the crews. He showed us a film of his ship rounding Cape Horn, with the teenaged sailors working under the most dreadful conditions, and I began to wonder why both he and Captain Johnson sailed always with young, untrained schoolboys when experienced sailors could have performed so much better. Was it because the heroic, tough sea captains with their huge ego and their domineering way were happy only when they had under their command youngsters whom they could terrify with impunity? We saw wretched boys clinging to the rigging during a gale. "I teach 'em to hang on by their eyebrows," he cried. "If they fall, they get run over." And he gloated that, when rounding the Horn, the cold sometimes tore out the boys' fingernails by the roots. "Better than having 'em manicured." "At times we have death aboard," he told us as we watched scenes of a funeral on his wildly tossing ship and the corpse sent into the waves, "but fortunately there is an inexhaustible supply of good young men; all you have to do is grab 'em."

The overfed, fat-bellied, cigar-smoking sedentary diners from Long Neck, New Canaan and Westchester vigorously applauded Captain Villiers. Many of them, I thought, had been provided with a vicarious thrill by the sight of all the good young men in the film who were so completely at the mercy of their cruel captain for so many months.

We also had with us, on the speakers' platform, the dashingly bearded Mr. Norman Baker, who twice crossed the Atlantic with Mr. Thor Heyerdahl in the reedboat *Ra* and who, by means of color slides, introduced us to his seven hunky companions on those scary journeys—each of different nationality but all heavily muscled and suntanned and bursting with vigor like the models in a male-order catalog catering to every taste. No wonder that, as he told us, he left a wife, three kids, a house with a mortgage, crabgrass and in-laws, to sail the ocean in such company.

Mr. Lowell Thomas, proud as a peacock in his golden jacket, rose to thank the speakers. The sailor blew his pipe again, the ballroom chandeliers lit up, menus were folded to be taken home as souvenirs, some slumbering gentlemen had to be roused by their table companions, and the evening with the boys was over—until a year later, when on April 14, 1972, Mr. Lindblad again took a table for twelve at the club's annual dinner at the Waldorf-Astoria and I was again one of his guests, as was the company's valued client Mr. Harley Quinn.

That year's chief attraction, at the end of the meal, was the appearance of Petty Officer Robert A. Croft, a United States Navy diver who was the first man in history to dive beyond two hundred feet in the ocean without any breathing device and remain there for more than two minutes. At a depth of forty feet, he had held his breath for six minutes and ten seconds, and this evening he was to give us a demonstration of the technique and discipline required to perform—and possibly to exceed—this remarkable feat.

A square glass tank filled with water was rolled on to the speakers' platform and a ladder was placed against it, by which Petty Officer Croft climbed up and lowered himself into the water. He was a rugged young man and wore a bathing suit of broad red and white horizontal stripes reaching from his neck to the upper arms and mid-thighs. A large underwater watch was strapped to his right wrist. Next to the water tank stood a dial around whose rim the numerals 0 to 59, to mark the seconds, were sufficiently large to be clearly seen from every part of the huge ballroom. When Petty Officer Croft had made himself comfortable in the water he raised his hand to show that he was ready to begin the demonstration and submerged his head, the dial's mechanism was set in motion and its single hand began to mark the elapsed seconds. When it returned to the 0 at the top of the dial, a ship's bell was rung and the toast master called out, "One minute!" while the hand moved around the dial to count off the next sixty seconds.

I was astonished—and so, I believe, were most of the dinner guests—how long one minute lasts. We watched in silence, spellbound, as the hand moved around the dial. The diver turned his head from side to side, smiled at the audience, moved his arms and legs, flexed his fingers and wriggled his toes.

"Two minutes!" called out the toast master.

The dinner guests became somewhat restive and no longer remained completely silent. In whispers and softly, they began to talk to those next to them, then to others across the wide tables. The waiters fussed about and refilled coffee cups, offered cigars and poured brandy.

"Three minutes!"

The table conversation became louder. Harley Quinn, sitting beside me, used the opportunity to question me about the travel arrangements I had made for his forthcoming trip to Rome, where he was to have a private audience with the Pope.

"Now then, honey, regarding those tickets to Rome. Of course ah'm *thrilled* to be interviewing the Holy Father, absolutely thrilled. Such an honor, honey. Now regarding mah tickets and vouchers: it says that ah'm to be met when ah arrive. But *where*? Oh, it says at the airport on arrival, but *where*? When ah went to see dahling Princess Grace in Monaco and our brave, brave boys in Vietnam, bless 'em, ah was met right by the plane, on what they call the tarmac, you know, and ah didn't have to go through all those horrid customs halls and all that. Is that what you've arranged for me? No? But where shall ah meet this C.I.T. man then? Ah must be looked after right, you know, because ah'm such a *child* when ah'm abroad, you've no idea what a child ah am. In America ah'm alright, you see, and of course mah chauffeur drives me to the airport in one of mah cars and meets me back there when ah come back; but when ah'm abroad ah'm lost, honey, lost like a *child*. So do get them to meet me right at the bottom of those horrid steep steps when the plane lands and see that ah'm looked after right. You've told them who ah am, haven't you, honey?"

"Four minutes!"

"And now regarding the Hassler-Villa Medici. Ah've got one of the rooms on the top floor facing St. Peter's, haven't ah? You've arranged that for me, haven't you, honey? Because it's quite *essential* that ah' have a room with a balcony and a view of St. Peter's. You see, ah'm going to begin mah article by saying 'Once more ah am in Rome, and this time to see the Holy Father. As ah draw the drapes of mah suite and step on to mah balcony high above the roofs of the Eternal City, there is the dome of St. Peter's before mah...'; and it must all be *true*, so you must send a telex at once and say 'Mr. Harley Quinn is a famous writer and his room must have a balcony with a view of St. Peter's,' and they must look after me right, and you can let them know that if ah'm really satisfied, ah'm even going to mention the name of the hotel in mah article. So send that telex and say 'Mr. Harley Quinn, the distinguished American writer, must have a room with a large balcony and view of St. Peter's,' because whatever ah write must be *true*, you see."

The ship's bell rang out and the toast master called out: "Five minutes!" but Harley Quinn did not let this interrupt his flow of trivia.

"Mah flights are by Pan Am in First Class, of course, but you've told them who ah am, haven't you? It's no good at all to be booked just as Mr. Quinn, that could be anybody. You must tell them that it's Mr. Harley Quinn, the influential writer, so that they'll look after me right. Because ah'm so used to be looked after right in mah apartment in New York, and in mah house in Connecticut, and by mah chauffeur and all mah staff, that ah'm quite *terrified* when ah go abroad unless ah know in advance that ah'm going to be looked after right all along. So you *will* tell the Hassler people and Pan Am that it's *me*, won't you, honey?"

The ship's bell sounded again. "Six minutes!" shouted the toast master and repeated: "*Six minutes!*"

By now everyone in the ballroom, except those diners who had fallen asleep, watched in complete silence as the dial hand marked the seconds. At six minutes and ten seconds, Petty Officer Croft's previous record, there was tremendous applause, ten seconds later the diver gave signs of being exhausted and at six minutes and twenty-three seconds he raised his head out of the water. He had beaten his record and accomplished an amazing feat. We had been privileged to witness history being made, and all the diners, even those who were befuddled by sleep, food and alcohol, gave the diver a standing ovation. He climbed out of the water tank, smiled at us, clasped his hands over his head like a winner after a boxing match, the toast master wrapped a blanket around him and he left the platform to continuing applause, hand-clapping and shouts of "Bravo! Bravo! Bravo!"

Despite the pandemonium in the ballroom, Harley Quinn's vapid mind continued to dwell on his travel arrangements, so much more important to him than having had to watch how long a common non-commissioned sailor in a 1920s swimsuit could breathe under water.

"So remember what ah told you, honey," he said, "and when ah'm back from Rome you shall have dinner with me at the Four Seasons, where a table by the pool is always reserved for me, and ah'll tell you what the Pope said to me. Ah'm told he's a perfect dahling."

Brian and I retained fond memories of our stay in Greenwich Village when we arrived to set up permanent residence in New York and where many of our friends lived, and whenever we went back there, to its interesting small specialty shops, to buy the aniseed pastries on which I doted from the Italian bakery on Bleecker Street, to dine at the intimate restaurants, to stroll along Christopher Street and across Washington Square and watch the chess players, we became increasingly convinced that this part of New York, with its easy-going ambience, was where we belonged.

We began to study the Real Estate section of the *New York Times* on Sunday mornings, where apartments for rent were conveniently listed by district and, after a few false starts, went to see one in a recently renovated early-nineteenth-century brick town house, part of a row, on Vandam Street, off Sixth Avenue three blocks south of Houston Street. One look sufficed: we immediately took it for a year's lease with option to renew. It was small, dark and low-ceilinged on the ground floor but had a truly spectacular, eighty-foot long private garden with forty-six well-tended rose bushes and many old trees, not only New York's ubiquitous ailanthus, but an oak, two pines, and a magnolia that was a stunning sight when in full bloom every May. From April to late October, we took all our meals out of doors at a trestle table and every August, when the display of roses was at its most magnificent, we gave an evening garden party for our friends and the office staff. Julie Garfield, the actress daughter of movie idol John Garfield, lived in the apartment above us and graced these festive occasions with her presence, as did the old Italian lady on the top floor, widow of the owner of the house, who often invited us to gargantuan, pungent meals, and our neighbor Leontyne Price, the opera diva, "one of America's national treasures," who one year delighted our guests when she walked among the roses and, unaccompanied, sang *Summertime*, her sensuous, plummy voice radiantly shimmering in the high notes.*

We felt completely at home, at last, more so than I had ever been in Hitler's Germany and in provincial South Africa, more so that Brian had been in his native Western Australia, where his preference for reading poetry over playing football was frowned upon, more so than either of us had been in caste-ridden England. When visiting, relatives and friends from Europe and Australia asked us: "How can you bear all the stress and noise and pressures of New York?" We found it difficult to convince them that our life was as tranquil and pleasant as if we lived in a small European village, from which we commuted on weekdays by subway to our office on 42nd Street high above Bryant Park—or, during public transportation strikes, hiked to and from it, covering the forty-five blocks each way in almost exactly forty-five minutes.

The mailman became a friend, not merely delivering letters (and far too many bills), but stopping for a gossip. The black appliance repairman told us about the Village men who summoned him to fix spurious problems and made passes at him (and seemed to regret that neither Brian nor I ever grasped the opportunity to do). Saturday mornings were particularly enjoyable, when I did our weekly shopping and the Irish butcher, the Italian baker, the Korean greengrocer, the Jamaican laundry owner all greeted me jovially. Watching the gay men cruising along

* I described this evening in my book *Volleyball with the Cuna Indians, and Other Gay Travel Adventures*, Viking Press, 1993.

Christopher Street, from the Hudson River to Sheridan Square, provided free entertainment all day and night. When Brian's sister Dinah from Western Australia visited us and we walked with her to a restaurant, she looked at all the tough, rough, athletic men in their denims and leather jackets and work boots sauntering up and down both sidewalks and innocently asked us if there was a large factory nearby that had just closed for the day and these men were its workers, streaming to the subway station to go home to their wives and families in the suburbs. When Mrs. Sonja Lindblad and her friend John Pugh, a British ambassador, came to the Village to make a round of the antique shops, on which we accompanied them, I was acutely embarrassed when one of Brian's and my most outrageous acquaintances greeted us and stopped to introduce his companion, whom he was leading on a chain and whose hands were shackled. "This is my slave Michael. Down on your knees, slave, and shake paws with the nice lady and gentleman!" he ordered. Sonja and the ambassador were stunned. "I guess that's the Village," she said as we walked away from the sinister leather-clad couple.

One Sunday, a Village neighbor, Mrs. Vera Schneider, organized a *Clean-Up of Morton Street Pier* on the Hudson River, where many local residents regularly gathered to sunbathe. Our Congresswomen, the feisty Mrs. Bella Abzug, wearing one of her wide-brimmed signature hats, came to lend us her encouragement and I was photographed with her. Ten years later, when Brian and I moved to Key West and our apartment was on the market, the realtor brought Mrs. Abzug and her husband to see it. Although they greatly admired the garden, the apartment was far too small for them, but she was enchanted when I pointed out the photograph on the bedroom wall of her, beautifully dressed, beside me, stripped to the waist for the clean-up.

Many of Brian's and my friends, men of our age, took delight in growing old disgracefully in the bars until four o'clock in the morning and then engaging in unspeakable activities among the trucks parked under the West Side elevated highway; but we enjoyed our quiet, sedate, village life and if we did venture into the turmoil of mid-Manhattan, it was to attend genteel, entirely respectable affairs such as the first meeting of the *Take a Teddy to Lunch Society* at the historic Algonquin Hotel at West 44th Street on January 18, 1982.

This frivolous fraternity was the inspired creation of the author and trendsetter Nancy Winters, who had enrolled me as one of the Society's charter members. The date for this luncheon was well chosen: it was a big week for teddy bears. Actor Peter Bull's teddy, Aloysius, made his American debut in the *Great Performances* series on Public Television, and it was also the 100th birthday of A. A. Milne, the creator of Winnie the Pooh. In England, flippant young men carried teddy bears around with them in emulation of Sebastian Flyte, the hero of Evelyn Waugh's *Brideshead Revisited*, and in the United States, young men displayed small teddy bears peeping out of the back pocket of their Levi's to denote that they were looking for cuddling partners. Prices of antique bears were soaring and collectors paid many hundreds of dollars for an authentic Steiff teddy with the distinctive metal clip in its ear.

The Algonquin Hotel's owner, Mr. Andrew Anspach, always avid to obtain good press coverage for his hotel and its guests, entered into the spirit of this bearish occasion properly to receive the *hug*, which is the correct name for a group of bears. The luncheon tables were festively decorated and there was a large selection of desserts to suit every ursine taste—honey cakes, coconut cakes, walnut creams. The charter members had been instructed to bring their teddys. Stephen Anderson, an Americana expert, carried a basketful of bears, large and small, sleek and furred; Erica Wilson, the current queen of needlepoint, had dressed her little bears in crocheted jackets and placed tiny rattles in their paws; a great-grandson of President Theodore Roosevelt, who had started the teddy bear craze when he spared the life of a young bear during one of his hunting trips, brought what he stated to be *the* original teddy bear; the cartoonist Gahan Wilson claimed that his many bears were snowbound in Connecticut but, being Nancy Winters' husband, he was not excluded from the luncheon. My somewhat battered old Steiff bear had accompanied me everywhere since my childhood, survived Hitler's holocaust and World War II, revolutions in two continents, earthquakes, hurricanes and shipwreck, circled the globe and lived with the monks at the Holy Mount Athos and with the Bedouins in their black goat-hair tents in the Sinai, hiked along the Inca Trail to Machu Picchu in the Peruvian Andes, crossed Greenland by dogsled, and sailed on the Amazon, the Sepik and the Nile. We were all photographed toasting the stars of the event, Aloysius and Winnie the Pooh, and, after having been featured in the New York papers as a scavenger of garbage cans, and as a sportive cyclist, I was now shown as the effete and ridiculous, middle-aged, proud possessor of a teddy bear.

Gahan Wilson portrayed me in a cartoon strip in *Mad Magazine* as the ruthless tour leader of *A Trip of a Lifetime* who conducted his unwilling victims on a journey of unmitigated horror, lampooning my offbeat tours and expeditions that were only occasionally very mildly hazardous. The protagonist of the strip was named Hanns von Hell and closely resembled me except that his gold ring was in his *left* ear; and I had to explain to Mr. Wilson that men of distinction throughout the ages invariably wore theirs in the right ear, as shown, for instance, in portraits of Elizabethan noblemen.

Since 1977, when I had bought a small house in Key West, Brian and I had spent one week there every month, until Brian remained there all winter and I commuted to and fro every weekend. After six years of so much traveling and with the costs involved in maintaining an apartment in New York and a house in Key West, we decided to move our travel company to Key West and to live there permanently. We had both loved every day and night in New York but it seemed that the time had come for us to move on. "But you *can't* go and live in Florida," our friends told us. "It's the waiting room to enter heaven." Well, maybe; but we hoped that we would be kept waiting at least twenty years.

Brian flew to Key West with our cat, to be there when the truck arrived with our furniture and clothes and our lares and penates, the spoils of our travels—wood figures from Easter Island, Papua New Guinea, Central America and Peru, Eskimo artifacts of caribou hide, Indian and Chinese temple carvings, ikons from Mount Athos and Amazonian palm frond baskets, our collection of Haitian paintings, and Brian's early Australian watercolors. I sold some remaining pieces of furniture to President Reagan's son, the ballet dancer Ronnie, who had recently married and was setting up home in Greenwich Village, and gave others away to friends and neighbors, so that I ended my stay in New York, after sixteen years, exactly as I had begun it, with nothing except one suitcase containing a few clothes and books and my teddy bear, and a mattress on the floor.

On the evening of Friday, March 25, 1983, I went around the corner for dinner at the cozy little restaurant where Brian and I had often eaten, and when I paid the check I said to the owner: "I'm sorry, but I'm never going to eat here again."

She was horrified. "Goodness, why not? What was wrong?"

"Nothing, but I'm moving to Key West, Florida, tomorrow morning."

She was greatly relieved. "You really had me worried," she said. "Good luck down there—but how can you bear to leave wonderful, wonderful New York?"

— 6 —

The Zoo in Manaus

In November of 1971, when I was still the vice president of Lindblad Travel, Inc., in New York (I resigned in July 1972 to start my own travel company), I was chosen to be a delegate at the Seminario de Turismo Amazonas in Manaus. Mr. Luis Zalamea, the North American head of the South American Travel Organization, had been appointed by Embratur, the Brazilian National Tourist Organization, to form a delegation from the United States to attend this seminar and wanted Lindblad Travel, Inc., to be represented because the *SS Lindblad Explorer* was scheduled to operate two cruises on the Amazon between Belem and Manaus in the following year. He assured me that the talks by the various officials, and the discussions at the working sessions on all aspects of Amazonian tourism, would be conducted in Portuguese but with instant amplified English translations.

When I checked in at John F. Kennedy Airport in New York for the flight via Bogota to Manaus, I learned that, apart from Mr. Zalamea and me, his North American Delegation consisted of only two other men whom I had not previously met—Mr. Robert Panero of the Hudson Institute, what was termed a "think tank," an expert on economic planning, and Mr. Paul Wright, son of the founder of Wright Way Tours in California, who specialized in travel to South America and who, in his early twenties, had first toured all of South America from Colombia to Patagonia on his motorcycle. He was now in his mid-forties, extremely garrulous and cheerful. We had only to look at each other for a moment to realize that we were birds of a feather and became instantly congenial.

Our arrival in Manaus was not propitious. The Embratur representative who was at the airport to meet Brazilian delegates on domestic flights from Belem, Rio de Janeiro and Sao Paulo did not have our names on his list. No *gringos* from North America were expected. Mr. Zalamea cursed and yelled abuse and threats, unaware that flies are not caught with vinegar but with honey. He and the Embratur man made many telephone calls, there were long delays and after an hour we were informed that, all hotels being full, accommodations had been secured for us on one of the ships in the harbor, which had been requisitioned for use by the Seminario delegates. A taxi was provided and took us to the *SS Lobo d'Amada* where, after a further delay, the ship's Embratur representative led us down to the lowest deck into a stiflingly hot, four-berth, inside cabin without a porthole. Communal washing facilities and toilets were three decks above.

Mr. Panero and Mr. Wright were aghast, and Mr. Zalameo was indignant. "They are insulting us!" he shouted and, there being no telephone aboard, hurried away to the harbormaster's office. We waited on deck, none too happy. Half an hour later, he returned triumphantly with a taxi; he had telephoned the Hotel Amazonas, the city's best, which was by no means fully booked, and reserved four rooms with private bathrooms for us—but as Embratur refused to pay for them; we would each have to pay.

Mr. Panero and Mr. Wright were delighted, but I told Mr. Zalamea that I would remain in the *Lobo d'Amada*, which caused him to vent an outburst of abuse on me. "*I* brought you here, and *I* am the head of the North American Delegation, and you will damn well do as *I* say!" I pointed out that it was not he who had brought me to Manaus but Embratur, and I felt that, as their guest, it was my duty to accept the accommodations they provided for me.

I returned to the bowels of the ship and made myself as comfortable as possible in the cabin, but when I went back on deck, I kept the key in my pocket so that Embratur could not inflict other delegates on me. I told the Embratur man that I would not have dinner on board but walk into town to see the famous opera house.

"Do not call it opera house. It is the Teatro Amazonas, and it is closed."

I said I would look at its exterior. I walked up the 450-foot-long ramp of the floating harbor and into the town.

To cope with forty feet of annual rise and fall of the waters of the Rio Negro, an entire harbor built on pontoons was created by Scottish engineers in 1902 and the yellow stones of the large customs building were brought from Scotland as ballast in ships coming to Manaus to collect the annual rubber crops.

One thousand miles from the Atlantic coast but only 100 feet above sea level, Manaus is located on high ground on the left bank of the Rio Negro, ten miles above the point where it joins the Rio Solimoes to form the Rio Amazon. In 1669, the Portuguese built a fort there and the garrison village was named Vila de Barro and traded in sarsaparilla, Brazil nuts and turtle-egg oil. It is the capital of the State of Amazonas, the largest state in Brazil and is surrounded by the vast Amazon jungle—only many years later did it become fashionable to refer to it instead as the *rain forest*—which begins only two miles from the city center.

In the mid-nineteenth-century, this insignificant settlement was transformed by the rubber boom, when enormous wealth turned it into a city renamed Manaus. Eduardo Ribero, the state governor in the 1870s, pronounced, "I found a village, and made of it a modern city."

The streets, a hundred feet wide, were laid out on a grid pattern and paved with cobblestones shipped from Portugal and eucalyptus trees imported from Australia to shade the main boulevards. There was electric power, a fresh-water plant, a race course, a bull ring, department stores, hotels and restaurants. The city was provided with telephone service in 1897, the same year in which the Teatro Amazonas was opened, having taken seventeen years to be completed. It has a dome of green, blue and yellow tiles and its magnificent gold-and-scarlet auditorium seats an audience of 650.

During the gilded age, the rich rubber barons built huge villas set in gardens behind high stone walls and in any architectural style they or their European architects fancied—English Tudor mansions, French and Italian baroque châteaux, Louisiana and Virginia plantation homes with Greek classical columns. But by 1912, when the rubber boom was over, the Teatro Amazonas was closed, the villas stood empty in their neglected gardens, the rubber barons' imported mistresses had departed, and Manaus had sunk back into poverty, misery and insignificance. Only the massive presence of the military kept it from oblivion. In 1971, it was estimated that of a population of half a million, less than seventy-two thousand were women; there were six men for every female.

Ever since the days of the rubber boom, when the only women were prostitutes and the mistresses of the rich barons, Manaus had the reputation of being strictly a man's town. No respectable Brazilian female would go there. Few of the men who were married could persuade their wives and daughters to live there with them, and those who did lived sequestered, as in a Muslim country, rarely left their houses, sent their servants to do the shopping and only showed themselves at church on Sundays, escorted by their menfolk. No females were employed in the post office, the banks, the offices of shipping companies and airlines; and as I walked towards the opera house—sorry, the Teatro Amazonas—I saw no women in the streets apart from prostitutes. The sidewalks were crowded with a slowly moving mass of men, almost all of them in a variety of uniforms, appraising one another with their eyes, turning back to continue their stroll with a companion.

The Teatro Amazonas was, of course, not closed, and although admittance to the orchestral concert in progress was free, few of the seats in the stalls were occupied; but when I looked up at the four rows of splendidly ornate boxes, I saw that they were filled to capacity. Apparently it was considered vulgar to sit in the stalls among the *hoi polloi*.

The exterior of the building was highly impressive, its great free-standing bulk surrounded by open spaces and low houses on all four sides, but its interior seemed to me to be more grandiose than that of any opera house I had seen. It alone had already made my visit to Manaus well worthwhile—and the local Embratur man had told me it was closed!

Next morning, the formal opening session of the Seminario—"suit and tie obligatory," I was instructed—was not held in that magnificent Teatro Amazonas but, as were all subsequent meetings, in the dreary auditorium of a technical school in a suburb. It was clear that Embratur was not only inefficient and ignorant but lacked imagination; and we four *gringos* were out of place among the four hundred Brazilian government officials, bankers, industrialists and eight State governors, who would all speak. It was not a tourism seminar but a political junket.

Not one of the delegates was female and none of the governors' and other officials' secretaries were women; but two haughty, elongated Amazons strode up and down in the lobby, and later along the aisle of the auditorium, with the assurance of giraffes. From their immensely high-heeled shoes to the tops of their coiffures piled up in the shape of beehives, these unattainable sex goddesses were over eight feet tall, dressed minimally in identical abbreviated skirts, slit at the sides, tightly-fitting, loosely crocheted tube tops, with matching leather shoulder bags swinging at their slim flanks and golden chains around necks, arms and ankles.

The delegates were wild with delight, but during their stately progress the pair looked neither left nor right. This brilliantly effective *coup de théâtre* had been devised for the titillation of the four hundred males by a Brazilian construction company, whose owner hoped to be awarded the government contract for building the planned motor road through five hundred miles of unexplored jungle from Manaus south to Porto Velho.

Brazil's minister of the interior gave the opening address at excruciating length and received tumultuous applause and a standing ovation when he ended, saying that the millions of Brazilians who traveled every year to the coasts in search of sun, sand and sex, must be persuaded instead to come to Amazonas because there they would find "*muito sol, muito areia, e muito sexo!*"

His address was not simultaneously translated into English, nor would any of the speeches and the discussions at the working sessions be translated, as Mr. Zalamea had told me, and as there was thus no purpose whatsoever in my attending them, I told him that I would instead use my time during the next four days to see as much as possible of Manaus and its surroundings. Mr. Panero and Mr. Wright were fluent in Spanish but could understand only very little Portuguese, and they said that they, too, would not attend. Mr. Zalamea was greatly displeased and accused me of being the instigator of this revolt. I became the black sheep of his delegation and at the seminario luncheons and dinners I attended, he snubbed me.

It was a joy for me to have Paul Wright with us. He knew Manaus well and offered to show me around. "Pick me up at the Hotel Amazonas at ten tonight and I'll take you to the most interesting places not listed in the guidebooks. Don't bring your wallet or your watch, and only very little money. The chief and flourishing industry here is crime and prostitution."

We walked around the harbor area, where rooms could be rented by the hour in the small hotels and through the park in front of the cathedral, under the tall ficus trees in the Avenida Sete de Setembro and then along the Avenida Epaminodas from the Military Academy to the Rio Negro Athletic Club. Everywhere we went we passed slowly strolling men, predominantly in the tight-fitting uniforms of the federal police, the city police, the marine police, the harbor police, different branches of the army, navy and air force, fire fighters, and officials of the duty free zone, the National Institute of Forest Development, the National Institute of Amazon Research. Paul identified them all by their uniforms and badges.

Slim, young men in black trousers and white shirts were waiters and barmen and hairdressers and office clerks. Many of them had thought to enhance their looks with facial makeup, eye shadow and false lashes, rouged cheeks and reddened lips, knowing that this rendered them more appealing to the macho military. They stood singly or in small groups on the sidewalk outside the many ice-cream parlors with cones in their hands sensuously licking their vanilla, strawberry or chocolate ices. Paul explained that those with chocolate ices had chosen them less for their flavor than to indicate that they favored Negroes or dark-skinned American Indians; vanilla ices denoted a predilection for fair, Nordic men.

"And the strawberry ices?" I asked.

"Oh, pink means any port in a storm," said Paul.

When the men in uniform spotted Paul and me, and any other rare tourist, they promptly ignored the painted local *maricones* and strutted to and fro before the visitors like peacocks, displaying their manly endowments under their thin pants. Foreigners had more money to spend to gratify their desires than waiters and office clerks, and the members of all the forces were so miserably paid that they could only rarely afford to buy an ice cream, much less a quarter of an hour in a side street or a park with a prostitute, and they were eager and willing to sell their favors to lonely men.

Next day, Paul invited me to drive some miles out of town with him to the Porta Negra beach, a mile of white sand along the Rio Negro, whose black water was very low. A few months later, as the river level rose forty feet, there would be no beach and both it and the forest for many hundreds of feet would be inundated. The Rio Negro's black water is free of sediments and silt and, despite its appearance, is perfectly pure. Humus and decomposing vegetation account for its dark color and high acidity which inhibits the reproduction and growth of insects, so that its shores are blissfully free of mosquitoes.

There were no women at the beach. The prostitutes of Manaus ply their trade only in the town and chiefly at night. Respectable women do not show themselves in public, particularly not on a beach frequented by the lowest class of men—the unemployed, disreputable members of soccer and athletic teams, branches of the underpaid military. Many of the young men at the beach remembered Paul from previous visits and gathered in a circle around us, talking suggestively in Portuguese or Spanish and trying out their sparse knowledge of English. Others pranced before us on the sand, showing off their fine physiques, played volleyball and soccer, did handstands, fell over each other and embraced and laughed.

"When I get to this beach, I always feel like a kid in a candy store," said Paul.

Brazil's population is wonderfully multiracial and the men, in their brief swimming trunks, so vibrant with health and vigor, were of all ethnic types—intensely black descendants of African slaves, men whose ancestors had come to the New World from all the countries around the Mediterranean, blond Scandinavians, Asians, Arabs and Jews. For the homosexual male visitor, Amazonas is indeed the proverbial Land of Cockayne, with choice examples of malehood available on display to suit everyone's taste. In 1885, when sexual activity between men could not be mentioned but was described in derogatory terms, the naturalist W. H. Hudson, traveling in Amazonas, wrote of the men there that they were "steeped to the lips in abominable vice."

"This sure is more fun than sitting through those dreary speeches at the Seminario," said Paul.

On the following days, when he was fully occupied morning, noon, afternoon and night with what he called "my many heavy dates," I set out alone to see the more prosaic sights of Manaus.

Early every morning I walked from the *Lobo d'Amada* to the Mercado Adolfo Lisboa, an extensive iron structure imported from France in 1902 and said to have been designed by Monsieur Eiffel. Here hundreds of small boats and canoes were jostled together at the riverbank, their owners shouting and arguing as they maneuvered their craft into the best positions to unload their fish. On long metal-topped tables, huge, bloated marine creatures lay disemboweled—manatees, cow-fish mammals, six feet long, their flesh considered to be more delicious than ham; dolphins almost as large, reputed to seduce young women and named the father of bastard children; equally big piracurus, whose meat is tasty both fresh and dried; brown tucunares with the distinctive black eye mark on their tails, whose fat is rendered down to be made into butter used in cooking. The small, notorious and voracious piranhas with their razor-sharp teeth were displayed in large baskets; their red variety is the most vicious and has the most delicate flavor. River snakes, fifteen feet long, lay on the tables being cut into slices, their bloody entrails retained and tossed into crates; eels of prodigious lengths and thickness were separated by size and expertly thrown alive into wooden barrels.

The chefs of the hotels and restaurants came here early in the morning to make their selections, and I watched priests and nuns in pairs, followed by Indian boys who carried baskets in which to take away their carefully chosen purchases. There were many small simple cafés, all well patronized, which offered nourishing breakfasts and at which I always seated myself as much as possible out of sight of the more repellent fish and snake carcasses. *Gringos* were rarely seen there and my presence aroused interest, and I learned quite a lot from those who were able to talk with me in English or German. It was most enjoyable to be there and savor the atmosphere and the company and the smells, but not a place for anyone who is squeamish.

I made a dutiful round of the city's museums and liked best the Museo do Indio, operated by Salesian missionaries, with astonishingly lovely and intricately woven baskets of different sizes and shapes, many of them for sale, and ceramics and wood utensils, garments in tapa and straw, and ritual objects of the tribes along the Rio Negro and its tributaries. The Museo Tirandentes, owned and staffed by the military police, housed historical items and sepia photographs of Manaus in the days of the rubber boom. The men were all dressed in immaculate white suits, starched shirts with high collars, ties and Panama hats, and the ladies of the town adorned in Paris gowns and feathered and flowered hats as large as cart wheels. Apart from a group of schoolchildren, I was the only visitor and the policemen were happy to show me around, indicating on their wristwatches at what time the museum closed and miming when they were free to meet me for a beer in the square opposite the museum.

One afternoon, I hired a motorized canoe with two sturdy boatmen to take me down the river to the Meeting of the Waters, where the black Rio Negro and the yellow-brown Solimoes run side by side for almost ten miles before their waters of different density and velocity begin to mingle in a highly spectacular manner and become the Rio Amazon.

Then Paul Wright invited me to drive two miles out of town with him to the edge of the jungle near the barracks of the 1st Jungle Infantry, where the Zoological Garden is maintained by COSAC, an elite unit of the Brazilian Army that specializes in training leaders for jungle combat and guerilla warfare. It is so well regarded internationally that the military from many other countries participate in its rugged, challenging courses.

When I met Paul in the lobby of the Hotel Amazonas, two taxis were waiting to drive us to the zoo and were to wait there for an hour and then take us back into town. He had also invited two effeminate hotel waiters and two young men from the Selvatur office to join us, and I was surprised how excited and thrilled they were by the prospect of making this nature excursion.

"Have you got money on you?" asked Paul.

I was puzzled why he asked me, and he elaborated. "Not just for your share of the cab fare and the entrance fee, but you'll need cash in the zoo."

I was still more puzzled. "But why? Do the animals have to be paid?" I asked.

This made him burst out laughing. "No, it's not for the animals," he said.

When the taxis arrived at the zoo, the infantryman on duty at the gate recognized Paul and called out "*Maricones*!" and sent another soldier to run to the nearby barracks and bring back at least six more.

I was totally perplexed and, as we walked into the zoo, asked Paul why so many soldiers were needed to guide us around, because I could see that most of the cages had signs with the animals' names.

"Don't be so naive, Hanns," he said. "I didn't invite you here to see the *animals*! We've come to make it with the soldiers, and they're all more than eager to entertain us. Six visitors in one afternoon is quite a windfall for them."

The hurriedly summoned contingent of soldiers arrived, sweating in their thin jungle fatigues, and Paul and the waiters and the travel agents strolled off, each with one or two of them, to secluded parts of the zoo. They did not glance at the animals; but I, not being as familiar with the Amazonian wildlife as they were, began to walk along the rows of cages and read the signs. Some animals that were harmless to man were not kept in the miserably small cages but roamed freely around and I allowed a few uncaged small monkeys to jump on my shoulders, and boldly put my hand through the wire netting to stroke a snake. The zoo contained more than three hundred animals of the region, and I saw three species of jaguars, tapirs, which are a cross between rhinoceros and horse, though much smaller, guinea-pig-like agoutis, copybaras with webbed feet, anteaters, opossum, and three-toed sloths with the uncanny ability to spend many days and nights hanging upside down from the branch of a tree, almost without moving. Among the larger and caged forest monkeys were the mapinguari, which abduct village women during the night and provide them with greater pleasure than their husbands, the tamorin which resemble squirrels, and the howling guaribas. In one fenced enclosure lay fearful reptiles—the greatly feared poisonous surututingo, ten feet long, the anaconda, largest snake in the world, thirty feet in length, which kills its prey by slow strangulation, and the boa constrictor, which is relatively harmless and non-poisonous but terrifying nonetheless.

I could not altogether avoid encountering Paul and the waiters and the travel agents as they enthusiastically coupled with the soldiers, and hurried away, but the uncaged tapirs and anteaters nonchalantly continued their slow perambulations and took no notice of the two-backed human beasts in action, a spectacle with which they were quite familiar.

The soldier who had insisted on accompanying me on my tour gave repeated signs of being disgusted and frustrated by the interest I showed in the animals and reptiles, but then he indicated by gestures that he wanted me to buy him a bottle of Coca Cola at the gate and, having drunk most of its contents, walked to a distant corner of the zoo and gave it to an anteater so that I could see how the animal lapped up the dregs at the bottom of the bottle with its incredibly long, thin tongue. Then he caught a monkey, held it fast with one hand and masturbated it with the other—a gross sight—and intimated that I should do the same to him. "*Eu sou um grande macaco,*" he said. I knew just enough Portuguese to understand what he meant.

Back at the gate, the soldiers showed themselves to be as well satisfied as the visitors, who had been generous in thanking them for their hospitality.

By the last day of the Seminario, Mr. Zalamea had realized that his three North American delegates felt they had been misled by him because none of the talks and discussions had been translated, so he arranged a special meeting, to be conducted in the English language, presided by Mr. Carlos Alberto de Andrade Pinto, the president of Embratur, and attended by approximately twenty Brazilian officials, hoteliers and travel agents.

While waiting in the conference room for the meeting to begin, Mr. Peter Schwabe, the owner of a large Brazilian travel organization, took me aside and attempted to persuade me to appoint his company to handle the shore excursions for the *SS Lindblad Explorer* cruises next year. I told him that those arrangements had already been finalized with Selvatur. "They are very incompetent people," he said, "and half of them are queers."

Mr. Pinto spoke perfect English, welcomed us on behalf of the Brazilian National Tourist Organization, and apologized for there having been no translations for our benefit. He was young, as handsome as a film actor, assured in manner, clever and adroit. It was clear that he had been appointed to head Embratur not only because he was, as Paul Wright whispered to me, the protegé and lover of Brazil's minister of finance, but in recognition of his ability and zest.

"Instead of having to go all the way to Las Vegas and Monte Carlo, four hundred Brazilian honeymoon couples will come each week here to our new Tropical Hotel Manaus and enjoy its lovely gardens and beaches, tennis and volleyball courts, swimming pools, restaurants and bars and night club, boutiques and sauna and beauty salons," he told us. Knowing how difficult it is to persuade just one couple to go to a hitherto unknown destination, I had considerable doubts that this would happen.

Mr. Pinta then asked the North American delegates to present their recommendations for developing tourism to the Amazon region.

Robert Panero spoke first and with confidence. From an economist's point of view, he explained, the Amazon region was a vast disaster area. The largest forest on earth provided no benefits except to a few monkeys and parrots. The largest river system on earth discharged fifty-eight-billion gallons of water per second into the Atlantic, like pouring it uselessly down a drain.

"A draconian measure is required to solve this dual problem of truly gigantic proportions," he said. A dam had to be built on the lower Rio Amazonas at its narrowest point, near Obidos, to form behind it a vast inland lake without the rise and fall of the river waters that at present made agricultural development along the banks impossible. Villages that would be inundated by the water of the lake would be relocated on higher ground, where millions of acres of unproductive forest would be cleared and the rich soil made available for the cultivation of three crops per year, as along the Nile. The hydroelectric power generated by the dam would produce sufficient energy for all Brazil's needs. The dam would prosper the whole region, which, instead of being a drain on Brazil's resources, would thrive and become the affluent heartland of the country and the economic wonder of the world.

Robert's listeners were stunned with disbelief as he pronounced his audacious plan. "Fascinating, quite fascinating," said Mr. Pinto.

"And so Manaus will disappear under the waters of your lake?" asked one of the Brazilian officials.

"Not at all. The dam will raise the water no more than ninety feet; Manaus is on higher ground and will remain intact and will be greatly benefited."

"And shipping, our major industry, will end because foreign ships can no longer come here?"

"Not at all. The dam will be equipped with locks to accommodate the largest ocean-going ships, in which they will be raised up into the lake and lowered from it as required. More ships will come to Manaus, larger ships, freighters and passenger ships bringing the thousands of tourists from all over the world who want to see this great modern technological achievement in operation."

I caught Mr. Pinto's quizzing eye and wanted to call out, "Damn the dam!" but prudence stopped me from doing so. It is always perilous to tamper with nature, and I liked the river and the forest as they were, always had been, and should remain forever.

Paul Wright struck a lighter note when he told us of his long association and love affair with South America. He was still relatively young, he said, but was looking forward to retiring before he became too old to enjoy himself, and when he did it would be in South America, in his favorite country, Brazil, in the place where he always felt most welcome and had many friends—in Manaus.*

Mr. Pinto and the Brazilian officials were highly gratified to hear this, and cheered him.

I began by saying that, although I had not attended the meetings of the Seminario because to my regret I did not yet speak and understand Portuguese, I had made good use of my time by exploring Manaus and all it has to offer a visitor. It seemed to me that Embratur did not sufficiently appreciate the unique appeal which Manaus and the Amazon forest exert on people in distant countries. I had been astonished, for instance, that a wonderful opportunity had been missed by not holding the meetings of the Seminario in the gorgeous gold-and-scarlet auditorium of the opera house—sorry, the Teatro Amazonas—a building that is as famous as the Taj Mahal and the Eiffel Tower. Their local representative had told me it was closed, but when I went there, I found a concert in progress. When I asked where I could hire a boat to take me to the Meeting of the Waters, Embratur said they could not help me, nor did they know the number of the buses that went to the Porta Negra beach. I did everything I wanted to do without their assistance. I had breakfasted in the *mercado*, had swum in the inky, clear Rio Negro, had obtained much useful information about Manaus, the river and the forest

* But some years later he chose instead to retire to Iquitos on the Amazon River in Peru, another gay man's candystore, where he acquired a fleet of passenger ships, the largest of which, the *SS Rio Amazonas,* I frequently chartered for my annual cruises for "intrepid gentlemen."

from the Salesians at the Museo do Indio and bought so many woven baskets that I did not know how I would get them all on the plane back to New York. I had visited the zoo and seen animals and reptiles and birds that were previously unknown to me. I had for a few days entered a world apart by itself that has no equal.

I explained why I thought it unwise of the authorities to try and attract Brazilian honeymoon couples to a resort with facilities that are found elsewhere, and ignore the attractions of the world's largest tropical forest with its unrivalled wildlife and flora, where trees rise to heights of 130 feet and more, the six-foot leaves of the floating *Vitória Régia* lily can support a child, where 1,500 species of fish live in the rivers and 1,800 species of butterflies, some with ten-inch wingspans, flutter through the foliage. And there are not only Mr. Panero's parrots but song birds, flamingoes, eagles and falcons, and a hundred varieties of edible fruits and fifteen-thousand species of insects.

I said that it was foreigners, not people of the country, who first venture to investigate and explore and marvel at rare sights, and quoted Francis Bacon who said four hundred years ago that travel in the young is education, in the old, experience. "Who," I asked, "can resist the opportunity to wander through the Amazonian forest with its novelty of plants, the beauty of its flowers, the tenuous vines, the luxuriance of all that vegetation? No wonder that Charles Darwin in 1836 said of it that to a person fond of natural history, progress through it on foot or by canoe brings with it a deeper pleasure than he can ever hope to experience again. And do not deprecate snobbism in tourism, but encourage it. Millions have heard about the mighty Amazon and Manaus and the rubber boom, but few have been here. Your minister of the interior said at the opening session that tourists will come here in search of sun, sand and sex; but no one from Miami, for instance, will come all the way to Manaus for something of which there is an abundance right at home."

I ended by saying that everything necessary to show the greatest forest on earth to travelers was already available. The army had planes and helicopters to take them deep into it, where they maintained lodges to accommodate them so that these people from London, Paris, Frankfurt, Stockholm, Tokyo, New York and Los Angeles could listen to the sounds of wildlife in the tropical nights under a million stars. Soldiers trained in jungle warfare were familiar with all aspects of the forest, knew its flora and fauna and could become informative and courteous guides for tourists, as some already were at the Zoological Garden, which they operated in Manaus.

Mr. Pinto had listened with attention to all I said and seemed astonished to hear how much I had done in Manaus during four days. Despite his duties at the Seminario, it was his pleasure to invite the North American delegates to luncheon, and with a nice touch of sarcasm he said that, since Mr. Ebensten knew so much more about Manaus than anyone else, perhaps he should select the restaurant. Everyone laughed and the irascible Mr. Zalamea became quite friendly towards me. A government limousine was waiting to take us to a garden restaurant on the outskirts of the town where he had ordered a delectable *caldeirada* for us, a richly flavored and nourishing regional stew with a selection of Amazonian fish, garden vegetables, and boiled eggs. The obnoxious Mr. Peter Schwabe and some others also joined us there, and when I declined the cocktails that were handed round, he said, "Aren't you man enough to accept a drink when it's offered to you?" After the meal, when we were given cigars, he addressed me again: "You don't drink, you don't smoke; you're not a man at all!"

Mr. Pinto honored me by seating me on his right. "So you went out to the zoo," he said, softly so as not to be overheard. "It is said to have some interesting attractions, but I am not personally acquainted with them. Did you enjoy your visit?"

I did not rise to the bait but merely replied that the zoo was indeed very interesting.

"Oh, no doubt. The fine fellows of our 1st Jungle Infantry have a certain reputation which has even reached me in Rio. Perhaps you found something there that is not in abundance in Miami?" He leered at me.

"Yes," I said. "There are no jaguars and tapirs and anteaters in Miami."

— 7 —

At Home in Key West

I first heard about Key West in 1962, when the perceptive British author, James Morris, wrote of it that "everywhere men are lazing about with no shirts on. It is a little city dedicated to easy living. At night, along Duval Street, a colorful crowd saunters and sips and gossips. In little cafés you can while away the hours listening to music and eating pungent Cuban sandwiches. Patio restaurants, in the courtyards of old houses, offer immensely long and varied meals. You can sip good wines and talk to artists, profane seamen, idlers, scientists and collectors of shells."

A year or so later, the *New York Times* described it as "a tropical resort that attracts a live-and-let-live breed for its blend of sun, salt, salubrity and a soupçon of sin," and I also saw a beautiful color photograph in *Time* magazine of two suntanned sailors in white bell-bottom pants, stripped to their waists, reclining on the floor of a room. The caption was, simply, *Sailors, Key West*—and what a surprise it was for me to learn in 1977, when I bought a small wooden house in the Old Town of Key West, that the photograph had been taken in Henry Faulkner's house, three doors from mine on Peacon Lane.

Henry was an eccentric, a painter and friend of Tennessee Williams, who walked around Key West singing in a falsetto voice accompanied by his pet goat Alice. When he died, he left his house to the son of the German playwright Bertolt Brecht, who rented its rooms individually to Will Soto, the lean, athletic wire-walker with the smile that still melts my heart, who performs at Mallory Square every evening, and to some of the others who entertained the tourists who gathered there to applaud when the sun set over the ocean—the Frenchman who made his cats jump through burning loops, the Living Statue in a Greek chitin and white body paint, the man who freed himself after being tied up in chains, fortune tellers and guitarists, singers of hymns, and the Iguana Man with whose hissing beasties intrepid visitors posed to be photographed.

Opposite, in the house in which he was born, lived the good-looking, genial retired policeman whose hobby was taking close-up photographs of the flowers of Key West's many tropical plants and trees. Directly opposite me lived a flight attendant who was having her large house entirely rebuilt, repainted, rewired and renovated by a succession of handsome handymen whom she never had to pay because they all shared her bed. When she introduced me to her latest live-in worker, an Englishman, and told me that he was a bricklayer but wonderfully expert at installing her new bathroom fittings, he reprimanded her: "Don't call me a bricklayer; I'm a master mason." I always knew where her airline had taken her when I found *The Times* of London, *Le Figaro*, Paris, or the *Frankfurter Zeitung* of the previous day on my front porch in the morning.

Next to her house was that of Lola Curry, a widow who lived alone and who became a good friend. She had been brought to that house from Cuba at the age of fourteen, knowing not a word of English, to marry a young man she had never seen and who was born in the house that was now mine. She never left the island, raised ten children, and had accumulated a huge collection of dolls in every possible material and of many ethnic types, who sat crowded together on all the chairs, settees, shelves and in cabinets of all the downstairs rooms and all the way up the stairs; I enjoyed adding to her family by bringing her dolls from the many foreign countries I visited. She told my friend Brian and me fascinating, occasionally indiscreet and ribald stories of life in Key West when she was young, gave us avocados and limes off her trees, and crocheted throw rugs for us. At the age of eighty-seven, after having lived in her house for seventy-three years, she was awoken one night by a burglar who viciously beat her before taking the small change in her bedside table. After this, her family insisted that she could no longer live alone and moved her to a nursing home, where we continued to keep in touch by letters and telephoning and where she died peacefully at the age of ninety-two. Her dolls all found good homes with her many grandchildren who each selected those they liked best.

Our nextdoor neighbor was—and still is—Walt Desel, a versatile painter who had been a major in the U.S. Marine Corps. His house bears a hand-lettered sign PEOPLE ON PEACON LANE DO NOT COMPLAIN and was the smallest gay guesthouse in Key West, advertised as "Where your fantasies come true."

Living in Key West was wonderfully easy, everything being within walking or cycling distance, strangers called out "Good morning" and "Have a nice day" to each other as they passed in the streets, and if Brian or I had a minor wound or a problem of the digestive system, we had only to cut a leaf off one of our aloe plants and rub the skin with it or drink its juice to be cured in no time.

We took pleasure in giving small dinner parties in our house. Brian brought back cookbooks and recipes from all his travels and became an enthusiastic and accomplished cook. He enjoyed planning and preparing Egyptian, Indian, Turkish, Peruvian and Polynesian meals as well as the classic dishes he had learned in the kitchens of the great chefs of France—Paul Bocuse, the Troisgros brothers and Madame Point—whose signed photographs graced the walls of our kitchen.

One of our most successful dinners was that which we gave to introduce Jan Morris to some of our local friends. She had not been in Key West since 1962 when she was still James Morris, and I arranged for Dennis Riley, "the Southernmost Bagpiper of the United States," who performed nightly at the sunset celebration at Mallory Square, to come striding down Peacon Lane and into our house in his kilt and full regalia, playing *Men of Harlech*. Jan, being a passionate Welsh patriot, was pleased with this, but a few months afterwards complained in a magazine article that Key West "suffers from a plethora of homosexuals." I could not let this pass unchallenged and argued that surely one can never have too much of a good thing. "Come off it, Hanns," she replied. "Can you eat strawberries and cream while listening to a Mozart flute concerto for twenty-four hours a day?" Her sentiment was echoed less politely fifteen years later by a young Australian relative of Brian's who, after staying with me for a week, wrote "Key West is flooded with ugly, fat, loud middle-aged couples and fags running around everywhere. Yuk!"

The only detriment to our otherwise contented existence was the nasty little monster who lived at the corner of Peacon Lane and Caroline Street and sold popcorn on Mallory Square at sunset. He was violently homophobic and put up signs on his house saying:

MAKE KEY WEST FAG FREE	and	STOP AIDS KILL FAGS

The latter sign had a picture of one stickman sodomizing another and was particularly offensive because three men living on the lane at that time were dying of AIDS.

I complained about the signs to the authorities at City Hall and they ordered them to be removed, which incensed the popcorn man even more. When Brian and I walked out of our lane into Caroline Street and he saw us, he shouted, "Walk out of the lane by the other end. I don't want to see you fags outside my house!" And he tried to run us down with his motorscooter and called out, "Out of my way, girls!" We were both approaching the age of sixty at the time. Later, he attempted unsuccessfully to become the city's mayor but received only forty votes. He would have been even more of a disaster than Captain Tony Tarracino, the owner of a raunchy bar with an unsavory record for drunkenness and gambling in New Jersey, who served as mayor for one term and whose campaign posters quoted him saying:

> ALL YOU NEED IN LIFE IS A TREMENDOUS SEX DRIVE AND A GREAT EGO—BRAINS DON'T MEAN A SHIT!

In 1819, Spain ceded Florida to the United States. In 1820, Commodore David Porter established a naval base in Key West to suppress piracy. He was greatly impressed with the island's location as a military and naval station and said of it that it had no equal except Gibraltar. Shipwrecks occurred daily on the treacherous reefs along the Florida Keys and wrecking was the chief occupation and made many early settlers rich. Experienced sponge divers came from the Bahamas and cigar makers from Cuba.

In 1912, Henry Flagler built the railroad that linked Key West to the mainland. By the 1920s, the Casa Marina, the La Concha and more than a dozen smaller hotels and inns provided 600 rooms for tourists, but the great hurricane of 1935 swept away the railroad and put an end to tourism. The sponging industry was ruined by disease. Only the navy continued to play a major role and sustain the city's economy until after World War II, when tourism revived and prosperity returned.

Members of families that first came to Key West in the 1820s—the Currys, Geigers, Porters, Roberts, Ottos—are as proud of their heritage as those in England whose ancestors arrived there with William the Conqueror in 1066 A.D. The symbol of Key West is the conch shell, and residents who are born there proudly refer to themselves as Conchs. The old wooden houses, raised on stilts off the ground to survive hurricanes and with pretty, frilly trim, are Conch Houses. Old cars, their sides often gaudily painted with representations of flowers, birds and fish, and so dilapidated as to be beyond repair yet still able to drag themselves wheezing along the streets, are Conch Cruisers. Bicycles in such ruinous condition that no one ever thinks of stealing them, are Conch Bikes.

The Conch families rule Key West, as they should, and although I feel more at home there than I have felt anywhere in my long life, I fully appreciate that I am and always will be an outsider. It surprises me when people who have lived there less years than I put themselves forward to tell the city authorities where to plant trees on sidewalks or in what colors buildings and the public buses should be painted.

In 1979, the Reverend Morris Wright of the Key West Baptist Temple launched a campaign to rid Key West of newcomers, in particular of homosexuals, and paid for advertisements in the local newspaper in which he announced:

> "If I were the chief of police, I would get me a hundred good men, give them each a baseball bat and have them walk down Duval Street and dare one of these freaks to stick his head over the edge of the sidewalk. You could easily get a hundred good men to serve in that capacity for a few hours. I know at least five hundred who would be only too happy to serve."

He went on to say that female impersonators and queers should be loaded into a deputy's automobile and shipped to the county line and told to get going back where such belonged. "Half of Duval Street is filled with disgusting, immoral, practically naked excuses for human beings. Say it can't be done? Yes it can. All we need is some good old-fashioned guts and morals."

A number of pious Baptist youths formed themselves into gangs, armed themselves with baseball bats and clubs, and followed patrons of the gay bars and the discotheque on Duval Street at night through the dark streets and attacked and injured them there. When these incidents became frequent, the owners of inns with a gay clientele organized unarmed patrols to escort their guests back to their lodgings. Tennessee Williams, Key West's most illustrious citizen, walking on Duval Street at night with his friend Dotson Rader, was beaten up but chose not to lodge a complaint, having been informed that among his attackers were the sons of several local police officers and firemen. "I like living here and want to continue to do so," he said.

The ensuing national—indeed international—press publicity was not beneficial to Key West tourism and the Tourist Development Association asked the Reverend Morris Wright to order his gangs to discontinue their persecution of tourists, who were spending much needed money in the city.

By no means did all Key West citizens approve of the good Baptist and the tactics by which he wanted to rid the town of "queers." Gay men, both residents and visitors, were overwhelmingly accepted and welcomed, providing that they behaved decently and with propriety. The gay men had learnt a bitter lesson and did not continue to behave in Key West as if it was *their* town. They were, and still are, only a small minority, and they no longer flaunted themselves so blatantly in public in what is a small and conservative town where families with children predominate.

I saw the good Baptist only once, in line at the Key West airport, where in deference to the somberly dressed and respectable old gentleman with his crew-cut gray hair and closely trimmed beard, he gestured me to pass before him through the gate. I said: "I am one of the queer freaks you wanted to be shipped to the county line, but I'm still here." He looked at me with surprise.

Key West became used to a great variety of visitors—hundreds of aspiring writers who attend the annual Literary Seminar; thousands of grossly overweight, beer-swilling bikers on their noisy three-day Poker Run and the almost equally overweight but far richer crew members of the competing teams for the even noisier three-day Powerboat Races; the Spring Breakers, four or more packed into every hotel room; the Women on the Water who are so sadly unfeminine; the elegant gentlemen from England and France who arrive in December to take up residence in their elegant houses for the winter; the athletic young men with the enigmatic words DIE YOUNG BROTHERHOOD tattooed on their backs.

Another campaign against a minority group was launched in December of 1988 by Miss Virginia Panico, a newcomer to Key West and one of the city commissioners. It was widely believed that she was in the pay of the owners of the large hotels, the Toppino Construction Company, and the Petrocelli Development Company, all members of a *cosa nostra* who wanted to gentrify the city and turn it into another Palm Beach exclusively for the very rich. In press interviews and on the radio and television she announced that she was going to ask her fellow commissioners to support her resolution to drive homeless people out of town and claimed that Duval Street business owners were "going berserk over these dirtbags."

"I want these people moved along. I want the police to harass them, to keep them up and moving, moving constantly, I demand that they do not allow these vagrants a moment's peace," she said.

I recognized in this woman from New Jersey a fascist who had studied the methods of Hitler and, by reviling a minority, aimed to acquire a solid following of like-minded haters to serve her ambitions. If her campaign against the defenseless homeless succeeded, she would be encouraged to turn her attention to gays, blacks or Jews. She had to be stopped.

I had never attended a meeting at the City Hall before, but did so on December 5 when her proposal was to be discussed.

"I own a travel company on Fleming Street, opposite a liquor store where many of the homeless people congregate," I said. "I see them every morning when I go to work and every afternoon when I leave my office and whenever I go to the post office and the bank and the beach. For many years, I have found them to be invariably polite and courteous. We say 'good morning' and 'have a nice day' to each other and I find them to be no trouble whatsoever. They are certainly not the people who want to assault me with baseball bats and drive me out of town, and they are not the owners of the bars whose loud amplified so-called music keeps me awake at night. Miss Panico tells us that tourists do not like them; but tourists do not photograph city commissioners, they photograph the picturesque homeless with their bright headscarves and straw hats and their guitars and dogs—just as they do not photograph Hyatt or Marriott hotels but dilapidated Conch Houses. Many of these people chose to live and sleep and eat in the streets—and even die in the streets, as we all know from what happened a week ago. In New York, the tourist sightseeing buses drive along the Bowery so that tourists can see them, in Paris they are called *clochards* and there are songs about them and postcards of them. Anatole France wrote of them: 'The law in its majesty allows the rich to sleep under the bridges of Paris, like the poor.'"

Although the mayor, at the start of the meeting, had warned speakers not to address their remarks directly to any commissioner, I did face Miss Panico and, unable to contain my rage, shouted: "Miss Panico, you are blessed with health and wealth and happiness; it is shocking that you want to harass these less fortunate people, want to keep them walking and walking, moving constantly, deny them a moment's peace. Do you want to drive them into the sea like rats? They are not rats, not 'dirtbags,' as you call them; they are human beings. People like them have always existed and always will. We must help them, stretch out our hands to them, not deny them peace. You say the merchants on Duval Street complain about them. At this time of the year, with Christmas approaching, you should remember that the merchants of Jerusalem complained about people just like them two thousand years ago—poor people, ragged, unkempt, with long hair, maybe not too clean—and the authorities crucified their leader and chased away the others. Have two thousand years of history taught you nothing? Have you no compassion? Have you no heart? Has greed made you totally shameless? Merry Christmas, Miss Panico."

When I concluded my speech, the mayor had difficulty in controlling the outburst of applause and stamping of feet. I felt completely drained and walked home.

I was enormously gratified by the public response to my speech. Strangers who had listened to the recording of the meeting on the local radio station congratulated me in the streets and at the supermarket and shook me by the hand. Three of the other city commissioners telephoned to thank me for what I had said. One told me, "This is the end of Virginia's ploy to become our next mayor." Police Chief Tom Webster in press interviews pointed out that Miss Panico was asking him to break the law. "You cannot arrest someone for being homeless, for being an alcoholic, for dressing a certain way, for smelling bad, for talking bad," he said. "That is unconstitutional, and I cannot violate people's civil rights."

Some of my friends thought that my verbal attack had been too cruel, but I argued that, by her outrageous statements and by calling on the police to break the law of the United States, Miss Panico had forfeited the right to be treated with respect. "One does not handle a rabid bitch with kid gloves," I said, "but uses every possible means to render the animal harmless."

To my delight, Miss Panico not only failed to become our mayor but was not re-elected as city commissioner. But she is a very smart cookie, and her supporters made her the president of the Chamber of Commerce, with a salary greatly in excess of that of the mayor and all the city commissioners combined.

The homeless in Key West are by no means all poor, but have sufficient incomes to enable them to live without responsibilities. I often envy them for their endless leisure while I, past my eightieth year, must still work long hours on five, six and often seven days a week to earn enough to pay the oncologist, the urologist, the dentist, the massage therapist, the trainer, as well as for medications, bus and taxi fares, food, utilities, household repairs, which in a tropical climate are essential and endless, taxes and insurance. The homeless often travel–to a cousin's wedding in Seattle, to a sister's graduation in Denver, to a college reunion in Chapel Hill–and in July, August and September, when they consider Key West to be too hot for comfort, to Cape Cod, Nantucket or Maine–and never by Greyhound bus, but always by air. I met many of them who bought their tickets from my travel company, and if they were $50 or $100 short, they were quite unconcerned and said they would easily raise the rest of the cash by next day–and always did so.

Americans are generous to a fault and do not insult any of those who sit or lie on the sidewalks, on the stone walls outside churches, and on the beaches, by giving them less than a dollar; five and ten dollar bills are not unknown contributions. As long ago as 1898, the visiting writer Stephen Crane, en route to the war in Cuba, gave a homeless boy in Key West fifty dollars. Those of them who squat where the tourists pass by and who weave hats with coconut palm leaves or strum guitars, each with his ubiquitous, well-fed dog beside him guarding the hat for contributions, make no less than two thousand dollars per month tax free, yet sleep at night in doorways or parked Conch Cruisers or on the beaches.

Many of them are highly educated, with university degrees, ex-military men qualified to fly planes and helicopters, licensed lawyers and architects. One evening when I walked past the convenience store on the corner of Peacon Lane, where many of them meet and buy wholesome bread, fruit, milk, beer and wine for their *al fresco* meals in the sun and enjoy their freedom and the company of their fellow outcasts, one of them called out, "Hey there, chief, where you headin' with that pretty lady?" To my very prim and snobbish cousin's consternation, I stopped and told him that I was taking my cousin from Paris out to dinner. To Ruth's astonishment, the ragged, unkempt creature addressed her in impeccable French and asked her for her opinion of the new and controversial glass pyramid at the Louvre museum. She was amazed.

"That's Key West," I told her.

Some of these happy idlers occasionally take on an easy job for an hour or so as laborers, making repairs, gardening, washing cars. One, who periodically trims the branches of trees in my garden that have grown too much and begin to interfere with the power and telephone lines, holds a degree in economics from Harvard University and discusses the novels of Jane Austen and articles in the latest issue of *The New Yorker* magazine. That's Key West.

Those who find living outdoors uncomfortable when the weather turns unusually cold in January or February, commit some petty crime in order to be arrested in the friendly manner of the city's police officers, so that they can luxuriate for a few weeks in the modern, well-appointed and heated jail, in its cozy cells with soft beds and ocean views, hot showers, a large selection of delicious dishes at the buffet meals three times daily, the television channel of their choice for entertainment, the use of a gymnasium to enhance their physique, medical check-ups, and congenial company. The vacationers staying at the Casa Marina or the Pier House Hotel and paying $400 per day are provided with less than all that.

The warm, languid air of Key West is conducive to persons who hatch impracticable and unrealistic schemes. There is the man who visited Cuba, became enamoured of young Cuban men, returned to Key West and collected money and medical and food supplies for Cuba, all of which would have been put to better use if he had donated them to the local branch of the Salvation Army. He shuttled for many years between Key West and Cuba and made efforts for them to be officially declared Sister Islands—but to make siblings of a little island four miles long with thirty-thousand people, and the island nation of Cuba, 2,500 miles long and with a population of more than ten million, was like proposing to mate a flee with an elephant.

Then there were the enthusiastic Key Westers who, in 1982, wanted the island to secede from the United States and become an autonomous Conch Republic, cheerfully ignoring the fact that the island is dependent on the mainland for its supplies of water and power and food. The mayor announced that he was now the first prime minister of the new republic; other ministerial posts and those of ambassadors in foreign countries were offered to the highest bidders. But what began in seriousness soon became a joke, with Conch Republic Days boisterously celebrated each year, and tourists avidly buy Conch Republic flags, T-shirts, car license plates and passports.

The houses of Conch families are closed to newcomers, but although my friend Brian and I were neither rich nor famous, we were invited once or twice during the fashionable winter season to garden parties at the houses of what in Key West is referred to as the A Set—people who cherish their privacy and at the rear of whose mansions are large, secluded gardens that cannot be seen from the street. Here the hired police guards at the front gate check invitation cards, the caterers' vans are parked by the side entrance, the reception line winds through the flower and antique-filled house to the lantern-lit garden, where hosts and guests screech with delight at seeing each other and the trio plays show tunes. Gentlemen in blazers and ladies in long chiffon dresses, their faces, necks and arms glowing with the deep tan of idleness, discuss the merits of their investments.

Brian and I were never a success there. As we wandered around the gardens, knowing almost no one, elderly *grande dames* on the lookout for presentable and obviously unmarried men, approached us and gushed: "Who *are* you—where have you *been*—I've never seen you here before—where do you live?"

We said that we lived on Peacon Lane.

"No, no—I mean where do you *really* live?"—because of course one only stays in one's house in Key West for a few weeks in the winter and really lives in one's brownstone in the East 70s in Manhattan or on one's estate in Connecticut or on Riverside Drive in Chicago or on the Ile St. Louis in Paris. To live in Key West all the year is social ruin, and when we admitted that we lived nowhere else, these ladies briskly turned their backs on us, cried "Betty—Herbie—how *are* you?" and strode away to greet friends of their own set.

A prominent winter resident who, before his retirement had been the head of a very large corporation, sent me a message through someone I know, inviting me to a cocktail party. I did not consider this to be a proper invitation and, in any case, dislike having to stand for an hour or more and talk with people I do not know, so, I declined. But two weeks later, this gentleman sent me a printed invitation to another of his prestigious cocktail parties, so that I felt flattered by his persistence and accepted. Two other guests drove me there. When the three of us arrived, the host appeared disconcerted and led us and three or four other gay men through his elegantly appointed mansion, past the bar and the lavish buffet, into the dark garden where there was no chair or bench on which to sit. There he left us and went back into the house to his heterosexual A Set guests—Key West's most floridly maquillaged real estate saleswoman and her obnoxious husband, the influential lawyer whose business dealings were being scrutinized by the Federal Bureau of Investigation, the leading lady of the city whose ancestors had amassed a fortune by wrecking, and other members of the local *beau monde*.

In this gay garden ghetto to which the homosexual guests had been relegated for fear of contaminating the real guests, I met a genial, middle-aged business executive who was accompanied by his new lover, Jim, a tousle-haired, broad-shouldered, tough young charmer from Atlanta with a suitably endearing Georgia accent. "I'm taking Jim with me across Asia," the elderly gentleman told me, and explained at length how they were going to start from Pakistan, traveling by local buses and hitching rides from truck-drivers, hiking across the Karakorum Desert and climbing up into the Pamir Mountains, sleeping in peasant huts or at wayside *khans* among dozens of vermin-infested Afghan nomads and heavily armed Khirgiz tribesmen and their livestock. They would make their way across several frontiers and the river Oxus to Samarkand and

Bokhara. "What an adventure we'll share!" he cried enthusiastically, looking adoringly at his new young friend.

Later, when I had boldly ventured out of the dark gay ghetto into the mansion and found myself beside Jim at the buffet, I said "What a great adventure you'll have in Asia! How I envy you!"

But tough young Jim was not looking forward with pleasure to that hazardous foray. "Mike likes all that," he glumly confided, "but my idea of roughing it is to stay at a Holiday Inn instead of the Ritz."

Another social occasion in which I had kindly been included but which I did not enjoy was a sunset cruise in my friend Del Brixey's motorboat. For more than twenty years, he had never invited me to join any of his cruises so I was quite surprised when he telephoned me one Sunday afternoon, apologized for giving me such short notice, and asked to join his cruise at 7:00 P.M. that evening. He had invited only authors! I hate being tossed about in a small boat and plied with alcohol, and I am not unaware that the sun sets every evening, but I accepted out of curiosity and when I boarded the *Miss Sunshine*, I understood that I had been asked because Del's other guests were six women authors, only three of them accompanied by husbands, and he wanted to have at least one extra man.

I knew only one of the authors, Annie Dillard, and had not seen her for twenty-eight years, when she was a member of one of my cruises to the Galapagos Islands. She looked as youthful and lovely as then and was nicely dressed; but, except for the biographer, Phyllis Rose, the other women had evidently never heard that it is the first duty of a woman to dress prettily. They looked like wretched, indigent bag-ladies, all well over sixty years of age. I had heard of none of these authors, although one boasted that 75 million copies of her books were currently in print.

We set off and immediately, vast amounts of alcoholic beverages were dispensed from a huge ice chest by Del's first mate. When the sun set, I thought that we would head back to shore and the agony of the cruise would be over—but Del turned on deafening disco sounds and the first mate climbed on to the ice chest and began to strip. Off came his belt, then his shirt, then he fumbled with the waistband of his shorts and I assumed that he had the ubiquitous jockeys under them, but no, there he was prancing about completely naked. I was not so much shocked (although I had never before seen a stripper in action) as embarrassed—what would all the women authors think of it?—but, one after another, they climbed on to the ice chest and hugged the stripper and fondled his genitalia and his buttocks to their hearts' content. Only Annie Dillard did not join in the action, either from a sense of decorum or because both her arthritic knees were bandaged. Five- and ten-dollar bills were thrown into the stripper's hat on the floor. I had come unprepared and had no money with me, but left an envelope with my contribution for the stripper at Del's house next morning.

The stripper, Peter, was from Zimbabwe, but not alas a big black stud.

He was thin and fair and his butter-colored body and the long, flaccid, uncircumcised tassel bouncing up and down between his legs did not appeal to me; I thought of what Dr. Samuel Johnson said about a dog walking on his hind legs, "It is not well done, but one is surprised to see it done at all."

But I had learned how the literary ladies of Key West spend their Sunday evenings.

I prefer the unpretentious hospitably of the good friends I have been fortunate to make in Key West–the male couples and the *ménages a trois* who like to cook–and do it well–and where the dinner tables by the pool are set with Meissen or Limoges china and there is always stimulating conversation and often bawdy gossip–and above all, the Rowan family, who bought Lola Curry's house on Peacon Lane after she had been robbed and assaulted in it. Her sons did not want to sell the house to a real estate speculator who might turn it into a rental property or accommodations for transients; they wanted it to continue to be the home of a family that would inhabit it through many generations. The Rowans–mother, father and four unusually well brought-up and well-behaved sons–tore the old house apart and, without professional assistance but great taste, themselves built what became virtually a new and beautiful example of the best in Conch houses. Father Bill, being a perfectionist, used only the finest and most durable materials, from the limestone block foundations to walls and floors of termite-resistant pressure-treated Dade County pine, to the 100-year old slate roofing tiles reclaimed from the Key West lighthouse keeper's quarters. He and the sons installed industrial waterproof plastic-shielded wiring throughout, and nineteenth-century doors rescued from other demolished Conch houses, including their original glass knobs. It took them more than five years to complete their labor of love, during which time they constantly apologized to their neighbors for the noise they made, but still had time to offer them and visiting relatives and friends their own blend of good-natured, easy-going convivial hospitality. Sheila is a perfectionist at the stove as Bill is at construction work, and she is quite unruffled when twenty or more people drop in for pot luck. None of the plates match, jam jars serve as glasses, some of the cutlery is family silver, some plastic, but the meals are always tasty, healthy, and abundant.

Brian and I grew very close to the Rowans and they honored us by letting us become part of their family. When Brian was ill while I had to go abroad to lead my company's tours, Sheila gave him all the proverbial tender loving care, and more—did his shopping, fed our cat, ran errands. During his last illness, in September 2001, when he was looked after with kindness and compassion by the doctors, nurses and staff at the excellent and well-equipped hospital that we are blessed to have on this small island, I do not know how I would have coped without her constant support. I will never be able to thank her sufficiently for being such a wonderfully supportive friend and neighbor. Brian and I had been a pair for forty-one years. As Horace Walpole wrote in 1776, lamenting on the death of his other self, John Chute: "Half is gone, the other remains solitary."

Until I moved to Key West, I had always lived in large cities with endless attractions, and my friends thought that I would be bored in a small town. But life in Key West is never dull and continues to provide me with surprises.

My greatest daily pleasure is to swim at 7:30 in the morning three or four times round the raft that is moored fifty feet off the Pier House Hotel beach in the Gulf of Mexico, and then walk back home for breakfast. One year, the Beach Club fee was doubled; I did not renew my membership and swam off the almost adjoining free beach at the bottom of Simonton Street where many of the homeless camp out all night. The water was the same but I never felt at ease there and friends who heard that I went to that beach facetiously asked, "What is the rich and famous Mr. Hanns Ebensten doing there among the dregs of humanity?" So I rejoined the Beach Club and enjoy my morning gossip with the staff and the use of the lounge chairs, the showers, the heated forty-feet pool in which I do twenty laps in mid-winter, when the ocean is often cold. The raft was the scene of an event that has become a Key West legend. Two carefree young men, high on drink and drugs and totally oblivious of their surroundings, were making love on it one afternoon in full view of the people on the beach and the terrace of the restaurant. The hotel management ordered one of the beach attendants to swim out and tell them to stop their activities immediately. "But why? No one can see us here!" they cried.

Each year I look forward to the hilarious Bed Race, much less publicized than the Fantasy Fest with its tawdry parades, but much more entertaining and unique. For this, four identically costumed members of the competing teams of hotels, guesthouses, bars, restaurants, the police and the firefighters, the hospital and the Coast Guard and many local business firms run as fast as they can down the length of Duval Street, pushing along an ingeniously decorated bed on wheels in which the fifth member of each team reclines as gracefully as the bed's motion permits and waves to the cheering crowd lining the sidewalks. I will never forget the sight of the pretty mother in the hospital bed, clutching her baby (a doll) as her four nurses rushed her to the finishing line.

A less amusing but novel learning experience was provided when my doctor (who even makes house calls!) sent me to see a specialist. I was superficially examined by a nurse and then led into the great man's room where he sat with his transvestite lover on his lap, using his letter opener to make lines of the cocaine spilled on his glass-topped desk. I had never seen this done before, only read about it, and looked away with embarrassment at the framed photographs on the wall, one of which was of a small railroad station in half-oriental, half-classical Greek style. I recognized it. "That's Yalta!" I said.

"Yes, my grandfather was the richest Jew in the Ukraine," said the great man, and he and his lover continued to sniff up the cocaine through straws.

I walked out and never saw him again, but two months later when I received my Medicare statement, it showed that they had paid the specialist $2,800 for services and treatments never supplied. He left Key West soon after this and no longer practices medicine.

Even having dinner at a restaurant with an acquaintance can bring a surprise. When a former football player came to Key West to apply for a job as one of my company's tour leaders, I took him to dinner at Claire's, a gay-owned establishment that was then the "in" place at which to be seen. He had achieved a certain fame when he revealed in his autobiography that he and his fellow athletes were often approached by rich elderly gay men who offered them hundreds of dollars for granting them sexual favors. The richest gay man in Key West, whose grandfather had bought much of its land in 1890 and who has appropriated the rights of a feudal lord, had been sitting at the bar, recognized the football idol and came over to our table and addressed him: "I can buy you a better meal than in this place. Let's go. My Rolls is parked just around the corner"—and Mr. David Kopay left me without a word of apology and followed him to his car.

Mr. Bob Crane, the owner of one of the most beautiful and truly civilized houses in Key West and who has cruised with me on the Amazon and the Nile, was appalled when I mentioned to him that, although I had lived in Key West for twenty-five years, I had never been to Fort Zachary Taylor. "This is ridiculous," he said, "You have been all over the world and you have never seen our best attraction, a mile from your house. I'll pick you up at three next Sunday and take you there."

A tremendous tropical rainstorm hit Key West next Sunday afternoon and people remained in front of their television sets, but Bob and I have reached the age when neither snow nor rain nor heat nor gloom of night stays us from doing what we want to do, so we were the only visitors. He is thoroughly familiar with the Fort Zachary Taylor Historic State Park and was an excellent guide. I was impressed by all he showed me and quite ashamed that I had never before gone to see that massive fort, which was begun in 1845 on orders of Commodore David Porter. Built of small hand-burned bricks on foundations of concrete, its sea wall was 225 feet long and 5 feet thick, and its original ten-inch Rodman and Columbiad cannons were still in place. It later became the U.S. Navy's submarine base and on its 87 acres of parkland, trees were introduced from U.S. Naval Stations in Panama, Guam, Hawaii and the Philippines. On a rocky promontory at the edge of the Atlantic ocean stand three life-sized metal figures of skeletal pirates, one complete with eye patch, guarding their treasure chest. They were created by Key West sculptor Larry Henke, who donated the group to the State Park in 1999 and gave the pirates whimsical names—*Dig Here*! *Found it*! and *Yippee*! Bob and I walked along the entire length of Key West's finest beach and watched a Coast

Guard patrol vessel plow through the ten-foot waves to assist a sailboat in distress. The gale-force wind lifted us off our feet and almost swept us to Cuba, ninety miles away. It was an exciting, informative, exhilarating afternoon in paradise.

When I discovered that the source of an unpleasant smell in a room of my house that I seldom use was due to my cat having urinated on the carpet, I sprayed deodorizing air freshener with baking soda, but with no success, and then lavishly treated it with the cutely named "Love my Carpet" that claims to get rid of any and all carpet odors. When this proved to be useless, I soaked the carpet in vinegar and put it to dry in the sun; but my darling Iswid had evidently soiled that carpet for so long, and so regularly, that nothing I did was successful in ridding it of its smell. It is a pretty Bessarabian carpet and was one of my first acquisitions for the house; and because it has a bright floral pattern, perhaps Iswid thought it was a field and that he was entitled to urinate on something so much more inviting than his mundane litterbox in the bathroom.

I carried the offending carpet to Universal Cleaners, where the sign beside the door shows a black cat licking her kitten's head and the slogan is GENTLE CLEANING. "I don't do carpets," said Joe Soldano, the owner, "and for sure none with cat's piss." But, helpful as always, he made me a gift of a small bag of his special non-bleach detergent and told me to go to the Kleen-Wash launderette where they have large 50 lb. washing machines. "Damn cat; you'll need plenty of quarters. Let me know next Saturday how you made out there!"

I have a washing machine at home, sufficiently large for my normal needs, but I had never been to a launderette and this was another new adventure for me, comparable to climbing to the ruins of Winay Wayna in the Andes by an unexplored route. I went first to change a five dollar bill at Fausto's Food Palace—"Not just a Grocery but a Social Center, since 1926"—where the NO SHIRTS, NO SHOES, NO SERVICE sign on the door is generally ignored, and then walked on to the Kleen-Wash launderette on Fleming Street, on the same block as four of Key West's most popular gay guesthouses. It, too, is a social center, and when the vacationing men at Coconut Grove, Coral Tree Inn, Curry House and the Oasis become bored with their fellow guests lying around the swimming pools and want to meet someone new and exciting, they take a few shirts or shorts to the Kleen-Wash, which conveniently shares premises with the Duds 'n' Suds Café, where the stools at the counter are so close together that strangers are forced to touch and converse, and which has tables and chairs on the sidewalk terrace. The comfortable, weathered wicker armchairs encourage customers to linger for hours over the café's fare, which comes in generous portions at prices that are amazingly low for Key West—sandwiches, Cuban beans on rice, chili and homemade soups in large bowls, beer, cold drinks, and *café con leche*.

Men from nearby guesthouses have been known to come here even without any laundry and sit for many hours happily watching the comings and goings of the customers, without the effort of having to trek across the island to the gay section of Fort Zachary Taylor beach. It is so easy here to make friends by asking, "Can you change a dollar?" or "Got a quarter for the phone?" because the public telephones require only 25 cents for a call anywhere within the United States, and the electronic blackjack machine also charges a quarter a game.

Notice boards display announcements for the cultural attractions of the town and gay snorkel trips to Man Key with Captain Del and Romantic Tropical Weddings performed by Marrying Sam "the 24-hour notary." Handwritten and typed notes offer rewards for finding lost cats and dogs, boats for sale, and cleaning and pet walking services. A vegetarian is searching for a room to rent. An artist is looking for models—"I have several paintings going at the beach, so you're likely to get a tan."

It was Saturday morning, not yet ten o'clock, and the place was almost deserted. The young men staying at the guesthouses were still asleep, having been at the gay bars and the discotheque until 4 A.M., and even the most industrious Key West residents who attend to their chores on Saturdays are rarely seen out before high noon. Respectable and affluent citizens are expected to have washing machines and dryers in their houses and it would be highly embarrassing for them to be seen at a public launderette, but if anyone who knew me saw me there, I was prepared to explain that my carpet with its obnoxious feline fragrance was too large to be washed at home.

I had expected there to be an attendant who would explain how to operate the washing machines, how to insert the quarters, which dials to turn and when, which levers to pull, but there was none. I asked the woman behind the counter whether there was anyone to assist me and she thought it was very strange that I had never used a public washing machine. A young man with blond hair in a straggly ponytail had been chatting with her as he drank a beer and laughed at my ignorance. "I'll show you," he said. "I'm Keith." We shook hands and I offered to buy him another beer. "Naw—I'm all right," he said. "Let's go."

He had strong arms and callused hands and wore scuffed yellow workboots, white sweatsocks, baggy khaki shorts that had been washed so often that they were bleached pleasantly to the color of bones, frayed and as thin, soft and inviting to the touch as a bedsheet, and a loose-fitting white T-shirt, also worn thin and none too clean—all of which are the ubiquitous garments of a hundred suntanned, ever-cheerful, attractive tousle-haired Key West carpenters, house painters, roofers, plumbers and yard workers. I liked his smile and decided that I would ask him to give me his telephone number; it would be useful to know an amiable handyman in the neighborhood. The delectable tropical climate of Key West is rough on the fragile old wooden houses, which need constant maintenance and frequent repairs. Termites and equally voracious wood-eating ants thrive; metal fittings rust; insect screens deteriorate; cockroaches invade and destroy electrical appliances. Roof gutters must be cleared of fallen leaves, cane chairs and kitchen and bathroom cabinets have to be mended, the garden gate needs a new lock, the front porch and railings are due for a fresh coat of paint, and the ever-encroaching bougainvillea has to be vigorously cut back outside the bedroom windows. I could keep a versatile handyman almost fully employed.

I produced the plastic bag with my supply of quarters and Keith was impressed by my efficiency. "You sure came well prepared." But how was I to know that the establishment provided a machine which ejected four quarters for every dollar bill it swallowed?

The cost of washing the carpet in one of the 50 lb. machines was stated to be $3.50. "You need seven quarters," said Keith and counted as I inserted them in the slot. Nothing happened. He opened and reclosed the glass door. Nothing happened. He banged the machine. Nothing happened. "You just lost your quarters," he said with calm resignation, but then I noticed a line of almost concealed lettering on the machine: INSERT 14 QUARTERS, it read. Of course, $3.50 is fourteen quarters, not seven, but I had been so enthralled by Keith's good looks and muscular body that I had not registered his mistake. I dropped seven more quarters into the machine and it began to revolve; together we watched until a red light blinked and then my helper poured in the detergent powder.

He sat his empty beer bottle on the top of the machine. "Now there's nothing else to do here for a half hour," he announced. "My place is right around the corner. I'll give you a good time. It's thirty bucks."

I was struck dumb with astonishment. My cheerful young helper was not a carpenter or a roofer or a gardener, but a hustler! Was this what Mr. Soldano, the dry cleaner, had meant when he told me to let him know how I "made out" at the Kleen-Wash launderette? Was it so well known as a place where the people bestowed their favors with such liberality? Had it been evening, I might perhaps have been less surprised, but this was 10:15 in the morning. I stammered out my excuses, my regrets at declining Keith's generous offer, for which I was totally unprepared. "Anyway, I only have this bag of quarters with me," I said mendaciously.

"No problem," said Keith and sauntered back to the café to resume talking with the woman behind the counter.

I watched my carpet being churned about in the machine, saw thickening soap suds obscure it from my view, waited for the first rinse, then the second, and calculated that if Keith turned ten tricks per day at his tempting low rate of thirty dollars per half-hour—and with his easy-going manner and honest, good looks—there was no reason why he should fail to do so—that amounted to more than $2,000 per week. Allowing for a two-week vacation to visit his folks on the farm in Iowa, it was $100,000 per year, tax free, without any travel expenses to and from his place of business and no standing about in smoke-filled bars or loitering in the rain on the streets or at the notorious Salt Ponds. How enviably easy is life for a young man as well-favored as Keith.

Other customers arrived, expertly changed their money and operated their machines, bought coffees or cold drinks and made themselves comfortable in the armchairs on the sidewalk terrace. Blond Keith sauntered among them and started conversations with the men who looked to him like possible clients, sat down beside them with his muscular legs thrust wide apart and made them laugh.

A light on my machine flashed. A buzzer sounded. Behind the circular glass panel, my carpet came to a halt. I pulled the lever to open the door and extracted it; it was almost dry and no longer smelled. I folded it and looked up, well pleased with the success of my mission, and stayed to study the people sitting at the counter of the café, bent over the blackjack machine or lounging in the chairs on the sidewalk. It was a delightful scene, a typically laid-back, warm, sunny mid-winter Saturday morning in Old Town, Key West.

There was shaggy-haired Jesse Riley, who had run barefoot across the United States, Australia and Asia, six-feet four-inches tall, waiting in line now to call his friends all over the country at the 25 cent rate. There, dragging along a huge plastic garbage bag of clothes, came the poet who lived on William Street in an abandoned car, whom God had endowed with the world's largest bosom, who changes her weird and exotic gowns three times daily and wanders around the town all day and night, reading aloud her verses. On a bench against the café wall, the perfect vantage point from which to observe everyone and gather ideas for his next book of scabrous tales, sat that burly, bearded bear, the author Leslie Pitteway, beer in hand, who was fond of saying, "I'm not gay, but I like to screw guys who are." At one of the tables, two youths—one an Asian with lovely shoulder-length black hair and a thong threaded with colored beads and feathers hanging from one ear—were starting the day with bowls of pungent chili and mugs of *café con leche.* Two big, black, interstate truckers sat on the ground playing with a kitten. The pedicab driver with a degree in anthropology had put his feet up on a table to rest them. But Keith the hustler had gone.

When one reaches one's eightieth year, one makes few new friends—and even fewer young ones. When I was introduced to a young, blithe spirit named Brad, I was bewildered by him; he was no earthling, not conceived by man, not born of woman. His ears did not hear what mine did, his eyes did not see what I saw. He and I inhabited the same planet but although his feet touched the earth, his head was up in the universe communicating with higher beings of which I had no understanding. He drank pure spring water and sparingly ate organically grown food, but received his spiritual nourishment from afar. He had no worldly possessions apart from a pair of frayed shorts, some batik sarongs, and a few tank tops. He owned no shoes, only leather thong sandals in order to be admitted into shops, the post office, airplanes. When he painted his toenails green, I could not resist telling him that I did not like it. "I didn't do it for you," he said, with perfect composure. He had no watch and did not know the day of the week or what month it was, yet in some magical way this did not prevent him from showing up at the airport every six weeks or so in time to be transported—not borne aloft by an eagle but mundanely aboard a jet airplane—to Siberia, where he ambled through the vast expanses of the taiga, unencumbered by clothes and subsisting on wild berries and roots; to Peru, where he paddled his own canoe along small streams in the Amazon rain forest, oblivious in his state of primeval nudity to attacks by ferocious biting insects; to participate in the tribal dances of the Shoshone Indians; and to Oregon, New Mexico and Tennessee to frolic naked with the Radical Faeries on the meadows of their sacred sanctuary lands.

In Key West, between these journeys in search of further enlightenment and spiritual fulfillment, Brad works as a naked gardener—not, he insists, in order to provide his employers with a salacious thrill, but because, as he says, "Life is a game, so why not play it naked?" This concept is quite foreign to me. My life has never been a game but a series of calamities, each of which I managed to survive by clinging to the wreckage in order to face the next; a striving, and a striving, a constant struggle during which I was at all times appropriately dressed, be it in blue jeans and a leather jacket, or a business suit and tie, or in boots and khaki pants and shirts when I climbed fearful mountains and crossed frigid deserts and hacked my way through tropical forests. It was always a challenge, never a game.

Brad does not know Chaucer, Tolstoy and Proust but writes as beautifully and poetically as they did, both in English and in Russian. Continuing acquaintance with him revealed other unsuspected accomplishments. In two minutes, he solved a mathematical problem connected with my writing which had puzzled me for a week. When I had a pain in my abdomen, he made me lie flat on the floor of my screened garden room, surrounded on three sides by soothing green foliage, bowed to the stone Buddha under the large banyan tree in my back garden, pressed the palms of his hands together and intoned *Namaste*, then sat cross-legged beside me and deeply inhaled the good air. His soul was released from his body and soared heavenward and he called upon the healing spirits and the guardian angels to ease me of my pain, and moved his hands over the afflicted spot; a beneficial life force entered me and half an hour later, the pain was gone. There are indeed more things in heaven and earth than I dreamt of in my philosophy.

In 1977, when my dear Brian and I bought our house in Key West, Brian planted a very small cutting of an Australian tree in front of the house, which he had brought back (illegally) from the Cape York Peninsula in Northern Queensland, where it is known by the natives as the Raki

Tali, "the red tree," due to its vivid red blossoms; its botanical name is *bracialiptus*. Twenty-five years later, it was more than forty feet tall and one of its branches was interfering with the telephone lines. I could not reach it by using my stepladder, and since Brad says there is no tree that he cannot climb, I asked him if he could cut off the branch. "Sure," he said, "but if so, I'll do it naked."

The tree is directly on the lane, but as there is almost no traffic and very few people walk there, I agreed. "But please be quick," I said.

He stripped off his shorts and climbed up, as nimble as a monkey. At that moment, a tourist came walking down the lane, intending to photograph the typical old Conch houses. He saw Brad in the tree and asked to take a picture; permission was granted, and then I was dismayed because a policeman appeared, to pay a social call on one of the tenants in the house opposite, but he merely gave the naked man in the tree a glance of complete indifference.

That's Key West.